Studies in African Literature

Art and Ideology in the African No~

Studies in African Literature

Art and Ideology in the African Novel

*A Study of the Influence of Marxism
on African Writing*

EMMANUEL NGARA
*Pro Vice-Chancellor and formerly
Head of the Department of English
University of Zimbabwe*

LONDON
HEINEMANN
IBADAN·NAIROBI

Heinemann Educational Books Ltd
22 Bedford Square, London WC1B 3HH
PMB 5205, Ibadan   PO Box 45314, Nairobi

EDINBURGH   MELBOURNE   AUCKLAND
SINGAPORE   KUALA LUMPUR
NEW DELHI   KINGSTON

Heinemann Educational Books Inc.
70 Court Street, Portsmouth, New Hampshire 03801, USA

© Emmanuel Ngara 1985
First published 1985
Reprinted 1987

British Library Cataloguing in Publication Data

Ngara, Emmanuel
    Art and ideology in the African novel.—
    (Studies in African literature)
    1. African fiction (English)—History and criticism
    I. Title   II. Series
    823   PR9344

    ISBN 0-435-91721-8

Set in 10/11 point Plantin by Georgia Origination, Liverpool
Printed and bound in Great Britain by
Biddles Ltd, Guildford and King's Lynn

Contents

▼▼▼▼▼▼▼▼▼▼▼▼▼▼▼▼▼▼▼▼▼▼▼▼▼▼▼▼▼▼▼

Preface

▼▼▼▼▼▼▼▼▼▼▼▼▼▼▼▼▼▼▼▼▼▼▼▼▼▼▼▼▼▼▼

African writers are constantly searching for a new social vision and new aesthetic standards. As shown in this volume, the writer is not only concerned with artistic forms but with ideological problems as well. Committed African writers are extremely sensitive to the social problems of their day and are constantly coming to grips with them, hoping to play their part in changing society for the better. They are therefore constantly defining the role of art in society and endeavouring to develop literary forms that match their social vision.

It is my view that if the critic is to perform his duties adequately he should in turn be sensitive to the concerns of the artist and develop critical norms which give a satisfactory account of the content and form of the art of the day. In my book *Stylistic Criticism and the African Novel* I tried to develop a theory of criticism which takes full account of the artist's concern with language and form in relation to ideological content. The burden of the present work is to search for critical norms which can adequately handle the problem of the relationship between art and ideology and enable the critic and student of literature to examine systematically the influence of Marxism on African writers. Ideology is therefore seen from two angles: the dominant ideology or competing ideologies of a society at a particular point in history on the one hand, and on the other the ideological stance of the writer. African artists find themselves producing their work in the context of certain ideological assumptions, and they consciously or unconsciously define their own positions in relation to these assumptions.

At present the philosophy that has in my opinion most adequately grappled with the difficult problem of ideology is Marxist philosophy, and it is my conviction that Marxist aesthetics offers a more profound understanding of the relationship between art and ideology than any other aesthetic in vogue today. However, for the critic of African literature, there are other reasons why Marxism and Marxist aesthetics should be of interest. In the first place, the influence of socialism globally and on the African continent in particular is becoming so significant that whether we subscribe to Marxism or not we would be ill-advised to ignore its impact on political, economic and cultural life. Politically and economically, a significant number of African countries have chosen the socialist path to development and the liberation movements of southern Africa are, in one way or another, allied to socialist countries which are much more prepared than the West to give them material assistance in the struggle against apartheid and colonialism. Consequently these liberation movements have adopted Marxism-Leninism as their guiding principle. The proliferation of Marxist ideas in Africa can be seen in the works of at least some African writers, including leading figures like Ngugi wa Thiong'o and Sembène Ousmane. That the influence of socialism is growing can also be seen from the fact that universities such as the National University of Lesotho are now prescribing courses on literature and socialism. Meanwhile, in western European countries Marxist aesthetics is increasingly becoming an important field of study, as witness the works of Henri Arvon, Louis Althusser, Raymond Williams, Terry Eagleton and others. All this points to the importance of introducing Marxist aesthetics to African students of literature, and to the necessity of a serious examination of the influence of Marxism on African writing.

While Marxist criticism is very rich in what it can reveal about content and ideology in literature, it has serious shortcomings in respect of its handling of the aesthetic component of a work of art. It is a *content-based* theory which, in its present state, cannot adequately account for the formal aspects of fiction. What is proposed here is a marriage of Marxist criticism and stylistic criticism, giving rise to what may be called *Marxist stylistic criticism*, where the principles of both Marxist aesthetics and stylistic criticism are applied consistently in the analysis of novels. In this connection it is necessary to note that the present volume extends the application of the theory of stylistic criticism. Whereas in *Stylistic Criticism and the African Novel* the theory was restricted to indigenous African writers of English expression, in the present volume we see its principles applied to works by mother-tongue speakers of the language (Nadine Gordimer and Alex La Guma) and to a novel translated from French (*God's Bits of Wood*).

I wish to submit that by applying the principles of Marxist aesthetics combined with the insights of stylistic criticism, we will be able to:

1. give an adequate explanation of the relationship between art and ideology;
2. explain the rise and development of modern African literature and the forces that gave rise to it;
3. examine the influence of socialism on the African novel and discover the ideological stance of the writer vis-à-vis socialism and other ideologies;
4. offer a satisfactory and balanced evaluation of the content and aesthetic quality of particular works of art.

The book falls into two parts. Part One, consisting of five chapters, presents a theoretical study of those aspects of Marxist aesthetics that are of direct relevance to this book. It defines and explains certain key concepts in their historical context, discusses the relationship between stylistic criticism and Marxist aesthetics as well as the problem of art and ideology, and gives an account of the rise and development of the African novel. Part Two, comprising six chapters, is an application of the principles articulated in Part One to the analysis of particular novels.

It is hoped that this book will give students and readers of literature a greater understanding of the functions of literature in society and will result in a deeper appreciation of the African writer's search for a new social order and new aesthetic forms.

E. A. Ngara

PART ONE
Theoretical Studies in Marxist Aesthetics

1 Marxist Aesthetics and Stylistic Criticism

▼▼▼▼▼▼▼▼▼▼▼▼▼▼▼▼▼▼▼▼▼▼▼▼▼▼▼▼▼▼

Marxist Aesthetics and Linguistic Approaches to Criticism

Since stylistic criticism is in a sense a linguistic approach to literature, it is incumbent upon us to open our discussion on stylistic criticism and Marxist criticism by referring to the relationship between the latter and linguistic approaches to literature, or what Yevgeny Basin calls 'semantic aesthetics.'

Basin emphasizes that from the Marxist-Leninist point of view the aesthetic study of art cannot be reduced to questions which are entirely soluble by the methods of such disciplines as mathematics, linguistics, semiotics and so on. Aesthetics should be seen in a much wider perspective: 'Aesthetics is concerned with problems of art as a whole, with questions of the nature of art, of the most general laws of its development, of the inter-relation of the material and spiritual sides of art, of the laws of creative artistic activity, of artistic cognition (reflection), of the assimilation of the outside world, etc.'[1] Basin contends that the semantic philosophy of art 'is characterized by a view of art as language.' And he goes on, 'The adherents of the semantic philosophy of art proceed from precisely this premise when they employ for their analysis of art the methods of such disciplines as semiotics, linguistics, systems analysis, etc.'[2] From the point of view of Marxist methodology 'this approach reveals an unmistakable metaphysical absolutization of one of the aspects of art.'[3]

But Basin admits that the semiotic, linguistic and other methods of analysis do present an important advance in the methodology of scientific study, since 'application of these methods makes it possible for art as the *object of study* to be represented in the form of different systems (linguistics, information theory, etc.) or, which comes to the same thing, in the form of different *subject-matters of study*.' Such an approach, he concludes, leads to a comprehensive analysis.[4] Here he touches on a fundamental principle of stylistic criticism. Spurning the subordination of form to content that is characteristic of conventional approaches to literary study and at the same time rejecting the narrowness of literary stylistics, stylistic criticism places content and form on an equal footing and holds that the *how* is as important as the *what* in genuine works of art. In this way it is possible to present a balanced and comprehensive analysis of a novel, to select all the significant aspects of an artefact and to do justice to them.[5] By emphasizing the equality of content and form, stylistic criticism thereby recognizes that sociological and aesthetic issues are of equal importance in literary study. Here, stylistic criticism parts company not only with conventional western criticism but also with Marxist criticism as commonly practised, for Marxist aesthetics is an aesthetics based on content with form playing a subordinate role, just as the superstructure is subordinate to the economic base.

I. A. Richards, one of the targets of Basin's criticisms, is accused of scientism. Scientism, Basin argues, is definable in terms of four characteristics: first, it reduces scientific information to information received by means of exact, quantitative methods; secondly, it absolutizes the role of scientific theories; thirdly, it declares the scientific attitude to be the only legitimate attitude to the world; and fourthly, it eliminates philosophy from the components of man's world view and metaphysical problems from scientific issues.[6] Scientism therefore consists in resorting to the sciences and scientific method only to the exclusion of philosophy and epistemology. Consequently, scientism is guilty of divorcing science from philosophy, and by reducing its analysis to a purely scientific method it fails to take into account the fact that there are disciplines such as literature which cannot be reduced to scientific analysis alone, and thus it suffers from narrowness and lack of comprehensiveness.

The same criticism is levelled against schools of thought which look at criticism from the point of view of linguistic analysis divorced from reference to content, and on the New Criticism of North America because of its formalistic emphasis on pure art and on art as an autonomous, closed structure unconnected to the real world around it.[7] I. A. Richards' theory of communication is naturalistic, Basin argues, because any sound and valid theory of critical analysis of art must take into account the fact that communication has a *social* and *historical* dimension. A scientific explanation of the nature of art is only possible 'on condition that the *common object* of artistic cognition ... is understood as the *communal* practice of feelings, which, in a work of art, moves from a dynamic to an existential or objective form.'[8] Art can be subjected to a scientific study 'only when it is considered as one of the vital functions of society in its inalienable connection with all the other spheres of the life of society and in its historical conventions.'[9]

Basin's criticisms of what he calls 'the semantic philosophy of art' are in the same vein as the objections of Marxist critics to the Formalistic School. This school of thought, which flourished in the Soviet Union soon after the October Revolution, was opposed to any form of sociological interpretation of a work of art and was characterized by an almost total disregard for content. As Arvon notes, 'the only thing of interest to the Formalistic critic is the poetic work itself, its composition, its rhythm, its metrics, and its style.'[10] In a characteristically anti-Marxist fashion, Formalism emphasized the autonomy of art and thus rejected the whole theory of the relationship between the economic base and the superstructure. In this way the Formalist School de-historicized art and emptied it of social meaning. The contradictions between Formalism and Marxist aesthetics were aptly summarized by Leon Trotsky when he said 'They (the Formalists) believe that "in the beginning was the Word." But we believe that in the beginning was the deed. The Word followed as its phonetic shadow.'[11] In everyday language this means that Formalism subordinates content to form and Marxism form to content.

Content and Form in Marxist Criticism

Terry Eagleton has pointed out that 'Marxist criticism has traditionally opposed all kinds of literary formalism, attacking that inbred attention to sheerly technical properties which robs literature of historical significance and reduces it to an aesthetic game.'[12] Small wonder therefore that the bulk of Marxist criticism focuses on content to the neglect of form. To cite only three examples among many, Lukács' pronouncements in works like *Studies in European Realism* and *Writer and Critic* are philosophical-sociological in the main. Lenin's famous essays on Tolstoy are almost entirely on the great writer's ideology, on Tolstoy as a mirror of the Russian revolution and Russian history, with hardly anything said about his style. The essays are an excellent analysis of Tolstoy's realistic depiction of the contradictions, conflicts and struggles of nineteenth-century Russia, but apart from a passing reference to the emotional power, passion and authenticity of Tolstoy's novels, the essays do not even begin to tell the reader how successful the novelist was from an aesthetic point of view. Christopher Caudwell's condemnation of Bernard Shaw's plays is completely based on the English playwright's bourgeois reformism, with no reference to his craft.[13]

There is indeed a sense in which the primacy of content must be conceded, and that is the fact that artistic forms are socially conditioned and issue from historical circumstances. Proceeding from this premise we are bound to conclude that a new content gives birth to a new form, meaning that form lags behind content. Furthermore, the majority of creative artists do not set out to write about the formal aspects of art; they set out to write about life, about society, about reality. It is this reality which they transform into artistic forms. That being the case we cannot argue for absolute equality between content and form. On the other hand we cannot rightly say that in every individual artistic production, content emerges as the dominant factor, even in the *effects* of the particular work of art. How does such a theory account for T. S. Eliot's poetry, whose incantatory power can have an overwhelming appeal on the reader while its semantic meaning still remains obscure and illusive? Is it only *what* Shakespeare says that makes him such a great writer, or *how* he says *what* he says? If it is a combination of the *what* and the *how* that makes great art, then the *how* should receive due attention in any theory of criticism that has a claim to comprehensiveness and adequacy. It is a major weakness of Marxist criticism that it does not pay sufficient attention to the *how* of particular works of art. This weakness has its source in Marxist-Leninist philosophy itself because of its emphasis on the primacy of the economic base over the superstructure and of labour over language. We shall return to the question of the relationship between the economic base and the superstructure in Chapter Three. Suffice it to mention here that in a work of art, content corresponds to the economic base and form to the superstructure.

That the exaggerated subordination of form to content by Marxist critics is not justified, even from the point of view of Marxism, is borne out by the fact that no less than one of the founders of Marxist aesthetics, Frederick Engels, later came to a realization of this deficiency and made what amounts to a serious confession. It is best to hear this straight from the horse's mouth. Commenting on Franz Mehring's book, *The Lessing Legend*, on 14 July 1893, Engels had this to say:

> This aspect of the matter, which I can only indicate here, we have all, I think, neglected more than it deserves. It is the old story: form is always neglected at first for content. As I say, I have done that too and the mistake has always struck me later. Hence I am not only far from reproaching you with this in any way – as the older of the guilty parties I certainly have no right to do so, on the contrary, but I would like all the same to draw your attention to this point for the future.[14]

This, he says earlier on in the same letter, is a point which 'Marx and I always failed to stress enough in our writings and in regard to which we are all guilty'. He and Marx laid emphasis on the *derivation* of ideological notions from the basic economic facts, he says, and then goes on: 'But at the same time we have on account of the content neglected the formal side – the manner in which these notions, etc., come about.'[15] This warning does not seem to have been sufficiently heeded in Marxist criticism as practised today.

Differences and Similarities Between Marxist Criticism and Stylistic Criticism

On the face of it, stylistic criticism has affinities with semantic aesthetics and linguistic approaches to the study of literature which Basin accuses of scientism. In the first place, stylistic criticism is a linguistic approach to literature. It seeks to bring the methods and insights of linguistics into literary criticism. For example, in accordance with linguistic practice, stylistic criticism aims at being more precise and more systematic than conventional bourgeois criticism. Accordingly it has a defined, basic critical terminology which lays down a set of evaluative criteria.[16] Secondly, it places much greater emphasis on the linguistic format or the language component of a work of art than does either conventional western criticism or Marxist criticism. It defines in linguistic terms the eight determinants of the linguistic format – in other words the factors which affect the writer's use of language in a novel – and divides the linguistic format into two well-defined sub-sets: linguistic features proper – sentences, words, metaphors, similes and so on – and para-linguistic affective devices like symbolism, myth and other forms of indirect reference.

But like Marxist criticism, stylistic criticism is opposed to scientism. It presents a radical departure from linguistic approaches to literature as defined in Yevgeny Basin's book and from a new branch of stylistics called literary stylistics, in that all these restrict their analysis to the level of language, to the total exclusion of the content of literature. Literary stylistics, for example, is restricted to the study of the language of literature. Raymond Chapman asserts that the sole concern of literary stylistics is style as a separate phenomenon from other elements of literature such as structure, theme and characterization.[17] On the contrary, the stylistic critic endeavours to avoid a purely technical approach to the study of literature and is as much interested in matters of aesthetic value and content as the conventional literary critic.

In common with Marxist aesthetics, stylistic criticism holds that in a realistic novel the content is socially conditioned and issues from historical circumstances, in that the subject matter of a work of art is a reflection of the writer's world.[18] Similarly, content is a determinant of form. The styles of Achebe, Okara and Armah in the novels analysed in *Stylistic Criticism and the African Novel* confirm the Marxist view that form is the result of historical conditions, that artistic form is related to social content. It is the conflict between African values and western values which has to a large extent determined the way these authors have used the English language in *The Voice, Arrow of God* and *Two Thousand Seasons*. The question they raise is: how can a foreign and colonial language be used to reflect African values? Thus Achebe uses Igbo modes of expression to reflect Igbo culture and also employs Pidgin and standard English in appropriate situations; Okara employs the method of transliteration to express African values; while Armah remoulds the English language so that it portrays Africans' views of themselves and their enemies. For this reason and in keeping with Marxist principles, the context in which a work of art is produced – the cultural, historical and geographical setting – is regarded as of crucial importance, being one of the major determinants of the linguistic format. Similarly the field of discourse or topic is seen as contributing to the writer's linguistic choices.[19] Lastly, stylistic criticism evaluates a work of art in terms of the following criteria:

1. Readability.
2. The appropriateness of the writer's linguistic choices.
3. The content value and aesthetic quality of the artistic creation as a whole, content and aesthetic quality being seen in dialectical interaction with each other.[20]

Here, content and form are put on an equal footing and the subordination of one to the other is rejected. Similarly, formalism and scientism are, by implication, rejected.

From the point of view of the social responsibility of literature, Marxist criticism as viewed by such theoreticians as Lukács, Caudwell and Brecht, and stylistic criticism share similar views for both see literature as a force of social change and liberation; and both aim at liberating the study of literature from the sterility and emptiness of bourgeois academicism. In my view the critic should both reflect the concerns and state of art, and help to shape and develop it. The critic is not merely an interpreter who simply tells us what Achebe or Ngugi says in his writings; the true critic participates in the creative process of the writer by helping to shape the intellectual climate of opinion in which art is produced, consumed and evaluated. It follows therefore that the literary theoreticians cannot meaningfully talk about the role of literature in a changing society unless they are concerned about man and society, unless they see themselves participating in the task of building a better and more humane social order, unless they are concerned about people's material and spiritual well-being.

With regard to Marxist criticism Eagleton has concluded his important book with the following words: 'Marxist criticism is not just an alternative technique for interpreting *Paradise Lost* or *Middlemarch*. It is part of our liberation from oppression, and that is why it is worth discussing at book length.'[21] It is this kind of view that Georg Lukács defends in *Writer and Critic*. Arguing that the development of capitalism and the consequent subordination of almost all the press to capitalist firms has transformed much criticism into an adjunct of the advertising apparatus of finance groups, Lukács contends that 'literary theoreticians and historians have abandoned all pretence at investigating the relationship between literature and society.'[22] In the hands of such literary theoreticians and historians, literature has been divorced from life: 'They treat literature as a circumscribed, autonomous discipline, and literature becomes, to use an over-simplification, a mere caricature and distorted reflection of certain superficial phenomena of the capitalist division of labour.'[23] This trend, Lukács suggests, has its origins in bourgeois sociology which has given rise to the abstractness and schematicism of 'sociological' literary criticism.[24] Such a trend is evidently anathema to genuine Marxist criticism and conflicts with the humanistic spirit of stylistic criticism.

There are, however, some important differences between Marxist criticism and stylistic criticism. Marxist aesthetics tends to subordinate form to content rather disproportionately. Although the emphasis on content insures Marxist aesthetics against the pitfalls of formalism and semantic aesthetics, and the narrowness of other linguistic approaches to literature by keeping the study of literature firmly rooted to reality, it nevertheless fails to do justice to the aesthetic component of individual works by paying insufficient attention to form. In the final analysis the critic must be able to account for the difference between reality as reflected in a work of art, and reality as depicted by social scientists such as historians, political scientists or sociologists. It is here that the Marxist critic can learn from the stylistic critic, for the latter aims at revealing how content is presented *in an artistic way* in genuine works of art, and he thus presents a balanced and comprehensive approach to the analysis of any particular novel. The comprehensiveness of stylistic criticism is coupled with a systematic method which enables the literary theoretician to carry out a satisfactory comparative study of different works by measuring them against a clearly defined set of parameters. In this way and by paying close attention to the text, the stylistic critic is able to avoid a purely impressionistic assessment of a novel, a pitfall into which Marxist criticism can easily fall.

On the other hand, stylistic criticism can be enriched by a more rigorous and consistent application of Marxist principles. A major advantage of Marxist criticism is what Henri Arvon has termed its 'global vision that seeks to encompass the entire field of reality,' its aim at totality,[25] as opposed to bourgeois approaches whose narrowness often lead to a shallow and uninspiring analysis of literature. It is this philosophical principle which enables the true Marxist critic to examine a work of art not only in terms of itself, but in relation to the totality of reality, human history, human relations and class struggles. It can help the stylistic critic to grapple more satisfactorily with the ideological dimension of a work of art and assist efforts to relate style to ideological content. Furthermore, because Marxism presents a dynamic interpretation of history, the nature of ideology, the category of consciousness, the structure of society and the nature of social struggles, critics can only benefit from the use of Marxist principles in their accounts of how these are presented in individual works.[26] Similarly, the application of Marxist principles will enable the critic to explain the ideological orientation of a writer and to distinguish between socialist art and non-socialist art.

Notes

1 Yevgeny Basin, *Semantic Philosophy of Art*, pp. 22–3.
2 Ibid., p. 23.
3 Ibid., p. 23.
4 Ibid., p. 23.
5 In actual practice the attention given to any aspect of a work of art and the time expended on it will depend on its relative importance in the novel.
6 Yevgeny Basin, op. cit., p. 29.
7 Ibid., p. 49.
8 Ibid., pp. 31–2.
9 Ibid., p. 48.
10 Henri Arvon, *Marxist Esthetics*, p. 64.
11 Trotsky, *Literature and Revolution*, p. 183.
12 See *Marxism and Literary Criticism*, p. 20.
13 See *Studies and Further Studies in A Dying Culture*.
14 See Marx and Engels, *On Literature and Art*, p. 66.
15 Ibid., p. 65.
16 See E. A. Ngara, *Stylistic Criticism and the African Novel*, pp. 22–34.

17 Chapman, *Linguistics and Literature: An Introduction to Literary Stylistics*, London, Edward Arnold.
18 See Ngara, op. cit., p. 15.
19 Ibid., pp. 19–20.
20 Ibid., p. 22.
21 See *Marxism and Literary Criticism*, p. 76.
22 Lukács, *Writer and Critic*, p. 197.
23 Ibid., p. 197.
24 Ibid., p. 198.
25 See *Marxist Esthetics*, p. 114.
26 See Chapter 3 of this book for an explanation of the terms 'ideology' and 'consciousness.'

2 Commitment, Realism and Socialist Art

▼▼▼▼▼▼▼▼▼▼▼▼▼▼▼▼▼▼▼▼▼▼▼▼▼▼▼▼▼▼▼▼

Views on Partisanship: From Marx to Mao

Socialism rejects the notion of art for art's sake in favour of the literature of commitment. So important is the problem of commitment and partisanship in socialist literature and Marxist criticism that it is necessary to open the discussion with an examination of the views of Marx and Engels on the matter.

In his letter to Minna Kautsky (1885), Engels states clearly that the socialist novelist does not have to declare openly his ideological position, and does not have to provide a solution to the problems of his day. All a socialist novel needs to do is shake the optimism of the bourgeoisie and instil doubt as to the eternal validity of their assumptions.[1] In a letter to Margaret Harkness (1888) Engels emphasizes the same point. There is no need to write a point-blank socialist novel, he says: 'The more the opinions of the author remain hidden, the better for the work of art.'[2] What he wishes to emphasize is the importance of realism which gives great artistic value to the works of Balzac and Tolstoy, who were by no means socialist.

It is, however, incorrect to construe from this that Marx and Engels were opposed to partisanship in literature. On the contrary they demanded that writers should project a progressive outlook in their works. 'I am by no means opposed to partisan poetry as such', Engels says, quoting Aeschylus, Aristophanes, Dante and others as partisan writers.[3] But the clearest example of Engels' approval of revolutionary art is his pronouncement on Heinrich Heine, 'The most eminent of all German poets', and author of *Song of the Silesian Weavers*. Heine's poem is a fiery and scathing criticism of 'Old Germany' with its 'blind and deaf god' and 'the King of the rich', a false fatherland where people 'suffered hunger and misery'. It is for this accursed Germany that the Silesian weavers are weaving a shroud 'with a triple curse.'[4] By contrast, Engels condemns Karl Beck who, in *The Poetry of True Socialism*, displays petty-bourgeois illusions and 'sings of the cowardly petty-bourgeois wretchedness...and not of the proud, threatening and revolutionary proletarian.'[5] Significantly enough, Engels takes the trouble to compare the ideological orientation of the two poets. He disdains Beck's petty bourgeois tendencies and lauds Heine's revolutionary fervour:

In Heine's case, the raptures of the bourgeoisie are deliberately high-pitched, so that they may equally deliberately then be brought down to earth with a bump; in Beck's case it is the poet himself who is associated with these fantasies and who naturally also suffers the consequences when he comes crashing down to earth. In the case of the one the bourgeoisie feels indignation at the poet's impertinence, in the case of the other reassurance at the attitudes of mind they have in common.[6]

Similarly, Engels applauds Georg Weerth, 'the German proletariat's first and most important poet' for his socialist and political poems.[7] The revolutionary poet must therefore take a partisan line and fire the bourgeoisie with his pen. It is their attack on the bourgeoisie which enabled the English realist novelists to make such a favourable impression on Karl Marx. These novelists – Dickens, Thackeray, Brontë and Gaskell – 'whose graphic and eloquent pages have issued to the world more political and social truths than have been uttered by all the professional politicians, publicists and moralists put together' impressed Marx because they criticized 'every section of the middle class', characterizing the class as 'full of presumption, affectation, petty tyranny and ignorance.'[8]

For Marx and Engels, partisanship necessarily demands that the writer be aware of history and class struggles. One of the criticisms levelled against Beck is that his poetry is typical of the poetry influenced by a German brand of socialism called 'true socialism.'[9] Now 'true socialism' is attacked in *The Communist Manifesto* for its inability to express the struggle of one class with another, for representing 'not the interests of the proletariat, but the interests of human nature, of Man in general, who belongs to no class, has no reality, who exists only in the misty realm of philosophical fantasy.'[10] Beck and other writers influenced by this school are characterized by shying away from history, by philosophical constructions and a vague outlook.[11]

What this discussion leads to, therefore, is the conclusion that Marx and Engels are not opposed to partisanship as such. What they are opposed to is the *method* employed by the author to express his commitment to the proletariat and his opposition to the bourgeoisie. What they object to is the open didacticism which Engels observed in Minna Kautsky's *The Old Ones and the New*. It is this open didacticism which he showed disapproval of when he wrote: 'You obviously felt a desire to take a public stand in your book, to testify to your convictions before the entire world. This has now been done; it is a stage you have passed through and need not repeat in this form.'[12] To this must be added that Engels was aware that the novelists of his time were addressing themselves to an enemy class, to the bourgeoisie, who were not sympathetic to socialism, and so, for tactical reasons, the revolutionary writer had to be less direct and try to affect the bourgeois consciousness unobtrusively without serving his ideology 'on a platter'.

For his part, Lenin stresses the subordination of literature to politics. The following passage from *Party Organization and Party Literature* is often quoted:

Down with non-partisan writers! Down with literary supermen! Literature must become *part* of the common cause of the proletariat, 'a cog and a screw' of one single great Social-Democratic mechanism set in motion by the entire politically-conscious vanguard of the entire working class. Literature must become a component of organized, planned and integrated Social-Democratic Party work.[13]

On the one hand Lenin is talking about Party literature only, on the other he includes imaginative literature as well. He categorically rejects the bourgeois concept of the freedom of the writer, artist or actress arguing that a writer cannot live in society and be free from it and that the bourgeois writer is not free from the bourgeois public and the bourgeois publisher. On the other hand the socialists will free literature from the bourgeoisie and link it to the proletariat:

> It will be a free literature, because the idea of socialism and sympathy with the working people, and not greed or careerism, will bring ever new forces to its ranks. It will be a free literature, because it will serve, not some satiated heroine, not the bored 'upper ten thousand', suffering from fatty degeneration, but the millions and tens of millions of working people – the flower of the country, its strength and its future.[14]

After the establishment of Soviet power in Russia there arose several literary movements in the country, notably the Formalists, the Futurists and the Proletkult. While the Formalists were more concerned with the formal aspects of literature than with its social and ideological content, the Futurists and the more politically influential Proletkult had a new vision of socialist art completely divorced from bourgeois art and dedicated to the aims of the working class. The Proletkult movement led to the formation of RAPP, the Russian Association of Proletarian Writers, whose goal was to create a new proletarian culture linked to the aims and ideology of the new socialist state and disdainful of the bourgeois past. This position is unacceptable to many genuine Marxists and is clearly out of line with that of Marx and Engels who recognized the value of good literature and art from classical times right down to nineteenth-century Europe. For his part, Trotsky, the writer of *Literature and Revolution*, advocated a more liberal approach to the arts and recognized the value of absorbing the more positive aspects of bourgeois art while pointing out the necessity of vigilant censorship in the creation of socialist art.

The move by Stalin and Zhdanov to bring writers under the control of the Communist Party resulted in the dissolution of RAPP and other independent literary associations and the creation of the Union of Soviet Writers in 1932. In 1934, at the First All-Union Congress of Soviet Writers, Socialist Realism, which urged all writers to be 'engineers of the human soul' and to see to it that literary creativity was part and parcel of Man's struggle against nature, was officially proclaimed as the guiding principle in Soviet literary endeavour. Reputed to have been coined by Stalin, the term is associated with Zhdanov, who was Stalin's spokesman, and Gorky, the first architect of socialist art now firmly in alliance with the ruling party. Here we see the notion of partisanship being reduced to a propagation of the official policies of a ruling political party, a position unacceptable to such Marxist critics as Lukács and Brecht, and one which can claim to be derived from the opinions of Lenin, but not from the pronouncements of Marx and Engels.

Mao Tse-Tung's views on the question of partisanship in art are similar to those of Lenin and are in part influenced by Lenin's. One can see why this is so. Both men were political leaders and each one of them formulated his views on the role of literature in society at the height of a revolutionary struggle, Lenin in the years preceding the October Revolution of 1917, and Mao at the Yenan Forum on Literature and Art in 1942, about seven years before the founding of the People's Republic of China. Like Lenin, Mao has very strong views on the partisan nature of literature. Having grouped the bulk of the Chinese population into four classes – workers, peasants, soldiers and petty bourgeoisie – he declares that literature should serve all four with the important proviso that: 'To serve them we must take the class stand of the proletariat and not that of the petty bourgeoisie. Today, writers who cling to an individualist petty bourgeois stand cannot truly serve the masses of revolutionary workers, peasants and soldiers.'[15] In Mao's view there is no such a thing as art for art's sake, for all literature and art belong to definite classes and serve definite political lines. Revolutionary literature is therefore subordinate to politics and should serve and influence the revolutionary cause: 'Revolutionary literature and art are part of the whole revolutionary cause, they are cogs and wheels in it ... they are indispensable cogs and wheels in the whole machine, an indispensable part of the entire revolutionary cause.'[16] It is the duty of the revolutionary writer, therefore, to produce works which awaken the masses, which fire them with enthusiasm so that they can unite in one single effort to transform their environment.[17]

If they are to produce such works of art, revolutionary writers must recognize that the people are the true source of literature. To create a genuine work of art writers must observe and study the people, their life, their struggles. They must study and analyse 'all the different kinds of people, all the classes, all the masses, all the vivid patterns of life and struggle, all the raw materials of art.'[18] They must do this because revolutionary literature 'should create a variety of characters out of real life and help the masses to propel history forward.'[19] By referring to real life Mao is emphasizing the importance of depicting characters and events concretely, and this is a fundamental principle of the Marxist conception of realism.

As the concept was first defined by the founders of Marxism we shall now turn to a discussion of their views on the subject.

Marx and Engels on Realism

For Marx and Engels, literary criticism hinges on the term 'realism.' The accurate depiction of reality is the most crucial aspect of a work of art. It is this

accurate depiction of reality which the founders of Marxism admired so much
in the works of Shakespeare, Dante, Dickens, Balzac and others. It is this that
gave lasting value to the works of these writers despite their ideological
orientation. Now how do we define realism?

The most cogent formulation of the term was made by Engels in his famous
letter to Margaret Harkness: 'Realism, to my mind, implies, besides truth of
detail, the truthful reproduction of typical characters under typical
circumstances.'[20] Realism therefore consists of three components: First, telling
the story truthfully and plainly, without 'artificial complications and adornments'; secondly, presenting *typical characters*; and thirdly, reproducing these
characters *under typical circumstances*. Margaret Harkness' book, *City Girl*,
fulfilled the first two criteria. The author told an old story but managed to make
it new 'by simply telling it truly;' giving it realistic truth. Its characters were
'typical enough' but – and this, to Engels, is where the author went wrong – 'the
circumstances which surround them and make them act, are not perhaps
equally so.'

Whereas the first two elements of realism refer to the manner of presentation,
to style and character, the third relates to the writer's awareness of history and
the class nature of society. Characters do not act in a vacuum. Their actions
derive from social and historical conditions and are reflective of the interests and
activities of a *class*. It is therefore the writer's duty to see what makes a particular
society in a particular historical moment tick, to see class struggles in their true
perspective and depict them accurately, showing how the actions of individual
characters are representative of classes making their impact on history. This is
where the *City Girl* failed, because 'the working class figures as a passive mass,
unable to help itself and not even showing (making) any attempt at striving to
help itself.'[21]

That one important element of realism is the writer's awareness of history and
class struggles comes out very clearly in Engels' letter to Ferdinand Lassalle in
1859. Praising the latter's drama, *Sickingen*, Engels has this to say: 'Your
Sickingen is on absolutely the right track; the main characters *are* representatives
of definite classes and trends and therefore of definite ideas of their time. They
find their motives not in petty individual lusts, but in the historical stream
which is carrying them along.'[22] Thus Lassalle was able to depict accurately the
official elements of the period of history he was dealing with; he was able to set
forth with great clarity 'the cities and the princes of that time.'[23] But as with
Margaret Harkness, Lassalle's analytical eye was not sharp enough to see the
historical importance of a lower rebellious class, in this case the peasantry. 'The
peasant movement was in its way just as national and just as opposed to the
princes as was that of the nobility, and the colossal dimensions of the struggle in
which it succumbed contrast very strongly with the readiness with which the
nobility, leaving Sickingen in the lurch, resigned itself to its historical calling,
that of flunkeys.' In Engels' opinion, therefore, 'the peasant movement deserves
closer attention.'[24]

But as Trotsky was to observe in *Literature and Revolution*, realism is neither revolutionary nor reactionary. To be able to see the class struggles of society a writer need not be ideologically radical, nor does he have to take sides with rebellious classes. 'The realism I allude to may crop out even in spite of the author's opinion.'[25] Thus Balzac was politically a Legitimist, a royalist, whose sympathies lay with the nobles, but he was at the same time a supreme example of nineteenth-century French realism: his works were so satirical as to suggest that the nobility was doomed to extinction. 'That Balzac was thus compelled to go against his own class sympathies and political prejudices, that he *saw* the necessity of the downfall of his favourite nobles, and described them as people deserving no better fate...that I consider one of the greatest triumphs of Realism, and one of the grandest features in old Balzac.'[26] Thus by its own dynamics realism compels a writer to present a progressive reflection of reality, even if this is against his own political inclinations.

Georg Lukács on Realism

Engels' definition of realism is most elaborately explained in the works of one of the major exponents of Marxist aesthetics, the Hungarian critic, Georg Lukács. It is useful at this juncture to refer to his views on several crucial aspects of realism before we go into the whole problem of socialist realism.

An important distinction which Lukács makes is that between realism on the one hand and naturalism on the other. The latter refers to a photographic representation of reality without penetrating to its essence. Here Lukács explains that while the crux of Marxist aesthetics is realism, 'it also combats vigorously any kind of naturalism and any direction which is satisfied with a photographic reproduction of the immediately perceptible superfice of the external world.'[27] True realism enables the writer to see the connection between things and to relate his description of objects to the essence of these objects and of the reality around them.

Marxist aesthetics, Lukács goes on, is also vehemently opposed to another false extreme in the theory of art: the view that since a photographic representation of reality is unacceptable, artistic forms must be seen as possessing their own autonomy, which means, in effect, that artistic creation and artistic forms are completely independent of reality and thus 'the artist has the right to transform and stylize reality at will.'[28] This view has been put across in a recent publication by Herbert Marcuse who believes in the separation of art from the process of material production, i.e. from the economic basis. 'Art has its own language,' Marcuse argues, 'and illuminates reality only through this other language.' And he goes on, 'Moreover art has its own dimension of affirmation and negation, a dimension which cannot be coordinated with the social process of production.'[29] To this Lukács would answer that 'the task of art is the truthful and accurate representation of the totality of reality.'[30] True art aims at a profound and comprehensive depiction of reality and does not present reality abstractly.

Another concept which is elaborated in the Lukács scheme of things is the type, in the sense of typical characters under typical circumstances. To Lukács the type does not mean archetypal figures of classical tragedy, neither does it mean 'the average.' The type, according to Lukács, means the convergence of 'all the most important social, moral and spiritual contradictions of a time.'[31] Through the discovery of typical characters and typical circumstances 'the most significant directions of social development obtain adequate artistic expression.'[32]

Like Engels, Lukács rejects the idea that the value of a work of art should be measured in terms of the writer's political ideology. But he confirms the view that the dynamics of realism compel the writer to present a progressive depiction of the conflicts of an epoch. Realism does not mean ideological indifference. On the contrary, 'there is a victory of realism only when great realist writers establish a profound and serious, if not fully conscious, association with a progressive current in the evolution of mankind.'[33] Thus Tolstoy, an aristocrat, found himself like Balzac alienated from his own class and depicting the struggles of the peasants against the inhumanity of their land-lords: 'Like all honest and gifted writers of the period, Tolstoy grew more and more estranged from the ruling class and found their life to an increasing degree sinful, meaningless, empty and inhuman.'[34]

Socialist Realism

Since the First All-Union Congress of Soviet Writers in August 1934, Soviet literary criticism has made a distinction between 'socialist realism' and 'critical realism'. Socialist realism is used with reference to Soviet literature starting with the works of Gorky, while critical realism is seen as the characteristic feature of the Russian and European realists of the nineteenth century, who 'absorbed the elements of democratic and socialist culture' in bourgeois society[35] and consequently championed the cause of the oppressed, and castigated capitalism, although they did not base their writings on the principles of socialism as such.

Maxim Gorky delivered a lengthy speech at the Congress in which he explained the difference between the two terms. The value of the works of critical realists, Gorky explained, was that they were models of technical excellence as literary forms, and they were also documents which explain the rise and decline of the bourgeoisie from a critical angle. The essence of critical realism, Gorky maintains, boils down to 'a struggle against the feudal conservatism that big business had revived, a struggle waged by organizing democracy, that is to say, the petty bourgeoisie, on the basis of liberal and humanitarian ideas, the organizing of democracy being understood by many writers and most readers as the need for defence both against the big bourgeoisie and ever-mounting pressure from the proletariat.'[36] This form of socialism, says Gorky, is only useful in so far as it helps to throw light upon the survivals of the past and helps socialist man to wage a struggle against those survivals and eradicate them, otherwise it cannot serve to educate socialist individuality. Socialist realism, on the other hand, 'proclaims that life is action, creativity, whose aim is the unfettered development of man's most valuable individual abilities for his victory over the forces of nature.' Socialist realism proclaims 'the great happiness of living on earth' which Man wishes to cultivate 'as a magnificent habitation of a mankind united in one family.'[37]

Socialist realism is therefore orientated towards the future, towards the building of a happy, successful and socialist society. The concept has been identified with Soviet criticism rather than with historical Marxist aesthetics and has been the subject of much adverse comment. Among the opponents of what may be regarded as a Stalinist conception of realism may be included Georg Lukács. Although he did not reject the term as such, he ended up projecting nineteenth-century realism, i.e. critical realism, as the model for all socialist writers to aspire to, a position not shared by other Marxist critics. Bertolt Brecht has vehemently criticized him for this because the Lukács position goes counter to Marxist philosophy by advocating a backward look to a past which was itself not socialist. However, as Eagleton puts it: 'There is no need to share the Communist Party's defence of socialist realism to endorse their criticism of the lameness of the Lukács position.'[38] Henri Arvon attributes the development of Lukács' position to the rise of fascism, a force that was seen by both socialists and westerners as a major threat to civilization and all mankind. The idea of forming a common front of the forces of socialism and democracy was being entertained by many Communists. In the literary arena, as the last chapter of *The Historical Novel* shows, Lukács was attempting to enlist on the side of socialism those bourgeois novelists whose critical realism could be reconciled to a socialist conception of the world, by the fact that their critical perception of bourgeois society could lead to a society free from the evils of the bourgeois world, i.e. to a socialist society. It was therefore important to emphasize the debt of proletarian culture to this progressive bourgeois culture.[39]

In the view of the present writer, there is a clear ideological distinction between socialist realism and critical realism, and this helps the reader and the critic to categorize works more satisfactorily. There is surely an ideological difference between Tolstoy's realism and Gorky's realism. And if such a difference does exist, a theoretical framework which enables the literary theoretician to account for the difference in critical terms is useful. However, because the term *socialist realism* is unfortunately shrouded in controversy, a controversy which the present writer does not wish to participate in, the operative word in this volume will be 'socialist art.'

The term *socialist art* will be used to refer to works which depict reality from a Marxist point of view, works which reflect the class structure of society and which present social struggles from the point of view of class and promote the ideals of socialism. In the words of Ernst Fischer, socialist art 'expresses the thoughts, feelings, moods, points of view and hopes of the new epoch and of its new class.'[40] As already pointed out, socialist literature is of necessity *committed* literature, committed to the building of a new society. Mikhail Khrapchenko has expressed the idea in these words: 'The building of socialist society, the emancipation of the creative forces of the people and the creation of conditions for the allround development of the potentialities and capabilities of the new man are the rich soil out of which the wonderful fruit of socialist art grows.'[41]

Examples of socialist art in the area of fiction are Maxim Gorky's *Mother* and the novels of the modern Russian writer Sholokhov, namely *And Quiet Flows the Don* and *Virgin Soil Upturned*. *Mother* was the first novel to present social conflicts in terms of the class struggle and from the point view of the proletariat. While *And Quiet Flows the Don* depicts modern Russian history in epic form from the days before the First World War to the consolidation of Soviet power and the defeat of the Whites by the Reds, *Virgin Soil Upturned* takes up the theme of the collectivization of agriculture in the Soviet Union, depicting realistically, with power and a sense of humour the problems and conflicts of different classes during that period of Russian history.

Notes

1 See Marx and Engels, *On Literature and Art*, p. 88.
2 Ibid., p. 91.
3 Ibid., p. 88.
4 Ibid., pp. 375–6.
5 Engels on Karl Beck, op. cit., p. 387.
6 Ibid., p. 388.
7 Ibid., pp. 402–5.
8 Marx and Engels on 'English Realists of the Mid-Nineteenth Century,' Ibid., p. 339.
9 Ibid., p. 389.
10 Marx and Engels, *Manifesto of the Communist Party*, p. 84.
11 Marx and Engels, *On Literature and Art*, p. 389.
12 Engels to Minna Kautsky, *On Literature and Art*, p. 88.
13 Lenin, *On Literature and Art*, p. 22.
14 Ibid., p. 25.
15 See 'Talks at the Yenan Forum on Literature and Art,' in *Selected Works of Mao Tse-Tung*, Vol. III, p. 77.
16 Ibid., p. 86.
17 Ibid., p. 82.
18 Ibid., pp. 81–2.
19 Ibid., p. 82.
20 See Marx and Engels, *On Literature and Art*, p. 90.
21 Ibid., p. 90.
22 Ibid., p. 103.
23 Ibid., p. 105.
24 Ibid., p. 105.

25 Ibid., p. 91.
26 Ibid., p. 92.
27 Georg Lukács, *Writer and Critic*, p. 75.
28 Ibid., p. 75.
29 See *The Aesthetic Dimension*, p. 22.
30 *Writer and Critic*, p. 76.
31 Ibid., p. 78.
32 Ibid., p. 78.
33 Ibid., p. 85.
34 *Studies in European Realism*, p. 147.
35 See Albert Belyaev, *The Ideological Struggle and Literature*, p. 185.
36 See Maxim Gorky, *On Literature*, p. 242.
37 Ibid., p. 264.
38 See *Marxism and Literary Criticism*, p. 53.
39 See Henri Arvon, *Marxist Esthetics*, p. 101.
40 *The Necessity of Art*, p. 180.
41 See 'Literature and Art in Today's World,' in *Social Sciences*, Vol. X, No. 3,
    1979, p. 102.

3 Literature, Society and Ideology

▼▼▼▼▼▼▼▼▼▼▼▼▼▼▼▼▼▼▼▼▼▼▼▼▼▼▼▼▼▼▼▼

Art, Consciousness and Ideology

In his polemical work, *Marxism and Literature*, Raymond Williams identifies at least three versions of the concept of ideology:

1. a system of beliefs characteristic of a particular class or group;
2. a system of illusory beliefs – false ideas or false consciousness – which can be contrasted with true or scientific knowledge;
3. the general process of the production of meanings and ideas.[1]

For the purpose of this book a simpler and more conventional definition of the term, amounting more or less to a combination of 1 and 2 above will be adopted. We will take ideology as referring to the dominant ideas of an epoch or class, with regard to politics and law, morality, religion, art and science. According to Marxist philosophy, social development is based on economic relations which constitute the material relations of people. But society also has an intellectual life which expresses itself in ideas and views about politics, morality, religion, art and science. All these are forms of consciousness which are dependent on the material economic relations of an epoch. In every epoch, therefore, there exists an economic base and a superstructure, the latter consisting of forms of social consciousness.

It is a fundamental tenet of historical materialism, on which the Marxist theory of social development is based, that *social being determines social consciousness*. In other words, it is not Man's ideas that determine his being, his material life, his economic relations in the process of producing wealth, but rather his being which determines his consciousness. Historical materialism holds that Man's history has progressed through various stages from primitive communalism through slave-owning societies and feudalism to capitalism and will finally progress to communism. In all these stages of social development, Man's social being is primary and his consciousness secondary. Before Man can engage in science, art or philosophy, he must work in order to get food, shelter and clothing. However, the superstructure influences the economic base; consequently ideology derives from the economic base and also influences it.

In class society, economic power is concentrated in the hands of a ruling class which controls the means of production. This same class also controls the means of mental production and consequently controls intellectual life. Hence the ideas of the ruling class are in every epoch the prevailing ideas, as Marx and Engels state in *The German Ideology*. Thus ideology has a class nature, or, as Lenin puts it in *What is To Be Done?*, 'in a society torn by class antagonisms there can never be a non-class or an above-class ideology.'[2]

Art is not in itself an ideology. As one of the forms of social consciousness, it has a particular relationship with ideology. This relationship, as Althusser would say, is not the same as the relationship between science and ideology. While science gives us a knowledge of reality, art makes us 'see', 'perceive' and 'feel' reality. 'What art makes us *see*, and therefore gives to us in the form of *"seeing"*, *"perceiving"* and *"feeling"* (which is not the form of *knowing*), is the *ideology* from which it is born, in which it bathes, from which it detaches itself as art, and to which it *alludes*.' It follows therefore that 'neither Balzac nor Solzhenitsyn gives us any *knowledge* of the world they describe, they only make us "see", "perceive" or "feel" the reality of the ideology of that world.'[3]

Literature enables us to see the nature of the ideology of an epoch because it is socially conditioned. In other words, works of art are basically reflections of particular social conditions and relationships. Although they have an autonomous existence and are produced by individuals who may hold divergent views about life, they have a more or less direct relationship with historical developments.

Literature and the Dominant Ideology of an Epoch

But if literature is socially conditioned and makes us see the ideology from which it is born, is it then always a reflection of the dominant ideology? In more precise terms, is the view of life expressed in the literature of all ages necessarily in harmony with the views of the ruling class which controls both the means of production and intellectual life? A look at a few examples will show that this is not always the case, that relations between literature and the dominant ideology are sometimes harmonious, sometimes in conflict with each other.

In traditional communities, art and society are at one. Songs, praise poems and folktales arise from the preoccupations, beliefs, assumptions and struggles of the community as a whole and are not regarded as creations of particular individuals. Thus African folktales express socially accepted ideas about goodness, virtue and bravery, while songs go with activities such as threshing, dancing, funeral services and religious ceremonies. In more advanced societies where the state has come into being and nations have been born and a class structure has emerged, we see literature being associated with the ruling class. Thus Ancient Egyptian poetry sings praises to the various dynasties; it immortalizes and deifies the Pharaohs, those powerful rulers of a slave-owning society.[4] In some West African societies kings and emperors employed *griots* to sing their exploits and extol their virtues and hand these treasures down from generation to generation. An example of this is the famous epic, *Sundiata*, which relates the heroic exploits of Sundiata, the founder of the ancient empire of Mali.

Other examples of harmonious relations between literature and the prevailing ideology can be seen in medieval Europe and particularly in Elizabethan England. In medieval Europe, the Catholic Church provided the dominant ideology, accepted by the various social classes of the time from the aristocracy downwards. The language of the Church – Latin – was also the language of education and the law courts, so that the Catholic clergy constituted the élite of the period, an élite that was in alliance with the ruling class. Not surprisingly, literature was placed at the service of religion. Medieval lyrics and the miracle plays such as *Everyman* provided a method of reinforcing the teaching of the Church in artistic form. This predominance of the Catholic Church was shattered by the rise of Protestantism with its emphasis on nationalism and, in consequence, the use of national languages.

The great Elizabethan dramatist, William Shakespeare, produced works that were capable of appealing to all sections of society in his own time and to different social classes in different ages and different lands. However Shakespeare was a child of his time, influenced by the prevailing ideology of his epoch, an epoch that held dear the notions of a well-ordered and stratified social system as well as the doctrine of the divine right of kings. His history plays, tragedies and Roman plays were about events which took place in times previous to Elizabethan England, but they were designed to illustrate the accepted dogmas of Shakespeare's own age. The doctrine of the divine right of kings held that a subject should not rise against his ruler. To do so was to disturb the natural and divinely-instituted order and could only result in chaos. Hence Macbeth should not have usurped power from Duncan; his actions resulted in the whole of Scotland being thrown into a catastrophic turmoil which only ended with the restoration of Duncan's line to power. Needless to say, artistic creations which fostered such views gave solace to the English monarchs and were therefore in harmony with their ideology.

The early English novel was in both form and content an expression of a new class – the bourgeoisie – a class that had overthrown the political and economic power of feudal lords in Europe and was rapidly imposing its own economic, political and social values upon a very large portion of mankind. The voyages of discovery, the conquest of foreign lands and the acquisition of raw materials from the conquered territories for the promotion of trade and industry were all undertaken by this powerful class, which at the same time broke asunder the communal beliefs and practices of feudalism and promoted the spirit of individualism in both economic endeavours and spiritual pursuits. Gone were the days of guilds and guild masters, and gone the times when only the established church had the right to interpret the Bible. Private enterprise was setting in and Protestantism was promoting the idea of religious freedom and freedom of conscience. Drama, which had been the dominant literary form of medieval and Renaissance Europe, could not adequately embody the new social content, the new ideology of the bourgeoisie. As Southall has argued, drama is public in performance because it appeals to a group rather than to an individual and was naturally the most appropriate form for the communalism of Europe.[5] Furthermore, the heroes of Shakespeare's plays are generally members of the ruling aristocratic class – kings and royal princes like Macbeth, Hamlet or Lear. With the rise of the bourgeoisie it was necessary to develop a literary genre that reflected the new ideology and the new economic system. Consequently the novel arose as an artistic form which could adequately project the values of the rising class – the spirit of adventure, individualism, and the acquisition and accumulation of wealth. And its typical hero was, naturally, a member of the middle class. But this is not to say that the early novel did not question the values of the bourgeoisie. Jonathan Swift's *Gulliver's Travels*, for instance, presents a shocking picture of the class by subjecting it to a sharp satirical analysis. However, if in its initial stages the novel genre threw overboard the values of feudalism and the Renaissance, it certainly promoted the ideology of the bourgeoisie. Thus Southall can correctly assert that *Robinson Crusoe* is 'the classic expression of the middle-class view. It gives something approaching epic status to that individualism which promoted and shaped the novel.'[6]

By the end of the nineteenth century, however, a wide chasm had developed between the ideas projected by the novel and the ideology of the ruling classes of Europe. This can be illustrated by citing the works of the great Russian novelist, Leo Tolstoy. As Lenin pointed out long ago, the works of Tolstoy were produced in the long period between 1861 and 1905.[7] During this period Tsarist Russia, a predominantly agricultural country which had lagged behind other major European nations in social and economic development, was experiencing a radical transformation from feudalism to capitalism. It was a time when the whole fabric of Tsarist society was crumbling down. The peasants were revolting against their feudal landlords, various ideologies such as nihilism were setting in, and the country was beginning to witness an unprecedented development in urbanization and industrialization, paving the way for the creation of a proletariat. *The Communist Manifesto* had been published in 1848 and Marxist ideas had gradually spread in both Russia and the West. In short, a new form of social consciousness was emerging in Europe, a consciousness hostile to bourgeois capitalism and one which found expression in the works of the realists of the West such as Charles Dickens and Emily Brontë and in the novels of the great Russian writers – Tolstoy, Dostoyevsky and Turgenev. In Turgenev, the discontent with the prevailing social conditions and the prevailing ideology is powerfully dramatized in *Fathers and Sons* where the forceful character Bazarov becomes an embodiment of the ideas of the nihilist movement, which was one symbol of the disintegration of the ideology fostered by the feudal-bourgeois regimes of the Tsars. Although himself a representative of the aristocracy, Tolstoy was able to reflect in his later novels the rise of the peasants against their landlords and was thus in the mainstream of European realists whose works presented a shattering critique of prevailing social conditions and the ideology of the ruling classes.

With the advance of the working class movement in Russia, the break betweeen the feudal-bourgeois ideology of the ruling classes and the ideology of the committed writer assumed unprecedented proportions. The major figure here is Maxim Gorky, who came into direct contact with the working class movement and got deeply involved in its activities. His writings were destined to play a major role in reflecting the struggle of the proletariat against Tsarist rule and in shaping the new social psychology. As Lukács has observed, Gorky 'stresses the dissolution of all the ideologies of old-time Russia.'[8] His novel *Mother* marks a crucial turning point in Russian literature and the literature of the entire world, for it is the first novel to depict the struggle against Tsarist rule from a partisan, working-class point of view. *Mother* and a subsequent novel, *Klim Samgin*, are deeply infused with the spirit of bolshevism which ultimately overthrew the old order and ushered in the first socialist state of the world in the wake of the October Revolution of 1917. Gorky's works accordingly present a complete break between literature and the ideology of the ruling classes.

Thus in nineteenth-century western and eastern Europe and early twentieth-century Russia we see a trend in literature which is unlike those trends referred to earlier on. There was now a clear contradiction between reality as presented by those who hold political and economic power, and reality as seen by the creative artist. This trend started with Romanticism, with its revulsion against industrialization and urbanization which were the concomitants of capitalist expansion. The trend shows itself in Wordsworth's poetry, in Blake's *Songs of Experience* and in the works of Byron and Shelley. Beginning with the works of this period, we see the writer questioning the dominant ideology of his era.

Adolfo Vázquez sees the modern writer as part of a trend which started with Romanticism, as having withdrawn from society and having become 'isolated and proscribed'.[9] This implies that the writer becomes a lonely figure, a voice crying in the wilderness. But is this really the case? Is the writer who shows aversion to the dominant assumptions of his age projecting a purely personal understanding of reality or is he the expression of a new and significant voice in his society? In the view of the present writer, Gorky, Tolstoy and Dickens are neither lone travellers nor isolated hermits. Theirs is an expression of a new challenge to the prevailing assumptions.

If they represent a significant social group or act as the focal point for voices of dissent, writers can sometimes be banished or tortured, as in the case of Alex La Guma and other South African writers who have had to flee from the land of their birth. Sometimes writers are pressured by the ruling classes into compromising their positions. In this way they become more acceptable, and at times compromise is the price a writer has to pay in order that his work may see the light of day. Thus in White-ruled Rhodesia, the Rhodesia Literature Bureau was faced with a dilemma between promoting the development of modern literature in African languages and ensuring that no writer openly criticized the status quo. Consequently, some writers had to water down their political stances before their work could be accepted for publication. In times of social upheaval, literature, like revolutionary music, can become a powerful weapon in the hands of those fighting for justice and human rights. Naturally, those in positions of power cannot disregard its influence on society and will, in certain circumstances, seek to contain it or direct its development.

The Soviet Union is a good example of how the state has sought to direct the development of literature through the formation of a writers' union and the formulation of a literary ideology, i.e. socialist realism. Without going into the question whether or not such a practice amounts to a 'regimentation' of the writer, we can certainly conclude that the fact that society can find it necessary to compel writers to form a union or to compromise their political positions is living testimony of the power of literature to influence history. It can be used as a weapon in defence of or against the existing social structure and to promote a cause. In colonial Rhodesia, Solomon Mutswairo's allegorical novel, *Feso*,[10] was regarded as an aid to political activity to the extent that some nationalists were reciting a poem from the book at political gatherings, with the result that the authorities did not hesitate to ban it.

What all this means is that literature, particularly committed literature, is not only a passive product of historical conditions, a passive reflection of reality, but it can also influence and help to shape reality; for literature is 'a social force which, with its emotional or ideological weight, shakes or moves people.'[11] There is therefore a complex and dialectical relationship between the economic base and forms of social consciousness such as art. The latter is more than a mere product of the former. As Lukács points out, 'Dialectics rejects the existence of any purely one-sided, cause-and-effect relationships; it recognizes in the simplest facts a complicated interaction of causes and effects.'[12]

Applied to the artist, this dictum means that the writer enjoys relative independence from history. Though a product of historical and social conditions, his own particular circumstances, his talent and intellect, his vision and degree of conciousness will all have a bearing on his art and can result in highly distinctive characteristics – within certain limits. It also means that the writers of an era will not present an identical reproduction of reality, although their works will all bear a relation to the dominant ideologies of the time. Each writer will express a certain 'view' of the ideology of his time, a view which may be predominantly socialistic, nationalistic, liberalistic and so on.

Literature, Nationalism and Revolutionary Consciousness

Although the dominant ideology of an epoch is that of the ruling class, there are times when different powerful ideologies co-exist in the same polity, but such is the nature of ideology that the coterminous existence of two powerful and opposing ideologies can only lead to the ascendancy of the one and the decline of the other. Kwame Nkrumah sees no peaceful coexistence between opposing ideologies in oppressive societies: 'There is such a thing as peaceful coexistence between states with different social systems; but as long as oppressive classes exist, there can be no such thing as peaceful coexistence between ideologies.'[13]

In times of crisis the dominant ideology can find itself facing a fierce challenge from a new ideology. This is true of nationalist uprisings whose whole thrust is a rejection of the forces of colonialism and imperialism and their attendant ideologies. The very nature of colonialism and imperialism inevitably leads to revolt by the colonized whose exploitation, dehumanization and enslavement sooner or later result in a national consciousness that openly challenges foreign domination. As Frantz Fanon has aptly put it, 'Colonial exploitation, poverty and endemic famine drive the native more and more to open, organized revolt. The necessity for an open and decisive breach is formed progressively and imperceptibly, and comes to be felt by the great majority of the people.'[14] Nationalism thus has the effect of raising the consciousness of subject peoples; it gradually opens the spiritual eyes of the oppressed so that they can begin to see that it is not right for a foreign power to subjugate them, and as they awaken to this new reality they also begin to reject the ideology of the ruling colonialists and to appreciate their own cultural values.

As we have already observed, literature can confirm or oppose the dominant ideology. The degree to which it confirms or opposes the dominant ideology depends on the degree to which the ruling class is challenged by revolutionary groups. Thus we can say that in feudal Europe there was no serious challenge to the authority of the Church, hence the literature of the period posed no challenge to the teaching of the Church and was in fact used as an instrument of the prevailing ideology. In times of nationalist uprisings, however, the dominant imperialist ideology faces a confrontation from the ideology of the rising national bourgeoisie which is often led by the intelligentsia. The conflict between nationalism and colonialism gives rise to tension in the ideological sphere, a tension between the pull of nationalism and the pull of imperialism, between the surging forward of the national democratic revolution and the holding back of acquisitive capitalism. Now this tension in turn results in a new form of art. 'All art is produced by this tension between changing social relations and outmoded consciousness,' says Christopher Caudwell.[15] At such crisis points, art is likely to present a significant challenge to the ideology of the ruling group.

But nationalism does not necessarily lead to a genuine transformation of society, because the national bourgeoisie often steps into the boots of the departed colonialists, maintaining the same old system and introducing only cosmetic changes, while working in alliance with the international bourgeoisie who control the economy of the country from a distance. So the workers and peasants, who had hoped to benefit from national independence, continue to be exploited under a new form of colonialism – neo-colonialism. The realization of this will often result in disillusionment among the masses who feel that they have been cheated by their new masters, the national bourgeoisie.

In the nationalist phase, when the struggle is seen as a fight against foreign domination, revolutionary art may arise, but the dominant theme will be that of nationalism which may find expression in 'decolonized' forms of English as in the case of Armah, Achebe and Okara and in literary ideologies like negritude, the African personality and other philosophies that are but the expression of the prevailing mood of nationalism. In the next phase, where the anger of the people is directed against bourgeois or feudal-bourgeois regimes, literature can get much more radicalized, presenting a sharp critique of both the local regime, whether military or civilian, and imperialism. A society which has entered this phase is ripe for the development of what Lukács calls 'revolutionary democracy' in the sphere of art.[16] It is periods such as these which produce novels of disillusionment typified by Armah's *The Beautyful Ones Are Not Yet Born*. Where the class struggle is intensified and class distinctions crystallized, socialist-orientated literature begins to emerge as happened in Maxim Gorky's Russia. Needless to say, the introduction of socialism leads to the development of socialist art.

But revolutionary literature does not only arise under conditions of socialism and in times of struggle against the national bourgeoisie after the liquidation of colonialism. There are times when nationalist struggles can give birth to such literature. It is a known fact that when nationalist struggles are prolonged they often become radicalized and Marxist-orientated. As the armed struggle intensifies in such situations, national consciousness also crystallizes and the psychology of workers, peasants, revolutionary intellectuals and other patriotic forces is transformed to a very high level of awareness. The liberation struggle assumes great significance in the thoughts and activities of an increasingly large number of people and those with literary talents use them to further the national cause. At this stage we get what Fanon calls 'a literature of combat,' a literature that calls on the people to fight for their existence as an independent nation. 'It is a literature of combat, because it moulds the national consciousness, giving it form and contours and flinging open before it new and boundless horizons.'[17] This type of literature expresses the will of a people to liberate itself from the shackles of colonialism.

It is not necessary to look very far to find examples of prolonged liberation struggles. We only need to refer to those African states which did not achieve independence in the 1950s and 1960s. These include the former Portuguese territories – Mozambique, Angola and Guinea-Bissau – Zimbabwe, and the last vestiges of colonial and racial domination in Africa, Namibia and South Africa. In Zimbabwe all negotiations with the colonial rulers failed until the principal nationalist parties, ZANU and ZAPU, abandoned the conference table and resorted to armed struggle in the bush. In this way the two organizations were transformed from nationalist parties to liberation movements, and as politics was radicalized the cultural sphere was revolutionized. Zimbabweans, young and old, wrote and composed revolutionary and Marxist-inspired poems and songs. An important feature of *The Voice of Zimbabwe* radio programme in Maputo was the singing and teaching of revolutionary songs, and, significantly enough, each broadcast concluded with the singing of the song *Kune Nzira dze Masoja*, 'the soldiers' code of behaviour,' which is a Shona rendering of Mao Tse-Tung's eight guiding points for guerrilla fighters.[18] In the literary sphere, the revolution inspired a rich and profound creativity which has given

Zimbabwe the volume entitled *And Now the Poets Speak* (Mambo Press 1981). The revolutionary consciousness that characterizes the volume is embodied in the poem which, in the words of the editors, is used 'as choric prelude' to the selection. In this poem entitled *Poem* Carlos Chombo, the author, sets out to define poetry in terms of African struggles, suffering and labour. This is the true source of revolutionary poetry. It is wrought by a people's resistance to 'effective occupation', by the massacres of masses fighting against colonialism and exploitation, by the torture and toils of people engaged in struggle. Here is the poem in full:

> The Real Poetry
> Was carved by centuries
> Of chains and whips
> It was written in the red streams
> Resisting the violence of
> 'Effective Occupation'
>
> It was engraved in killings in Katanga,
> In the betrayals of Mau-Mau,
> In the countless anti-people coups
>
> Its beat was the bones in Bissau
> Its metaphors massacres in Mozambique
> Its alliterations agony in Angola
> Its form and zenith
> Fighting in Zimbabwe
>
> The Real Poetry
> Is sweat scouring
> The baked valley of the peasant's back
> Down to the starved gorge of his buttocks
>
> It bubbles and boils
> In the blisters of the farm labourer
>
> It glides in the greased hands
> Of the factory worker
>
> Not a private paradise
> Nor an individual inferno
>
> But the pain and pleasure
> Of People in Struggle
>
> *Vivo O Povo!*[19]

There are echoes of Agostinho Neto here, whose poetry was influenced by a similar struggle in Angola. This is a poetry of revolt, a poetry which expresses a new social psychology, a new consciousness of a people at the height of a revolution. In South Africa, where the nationalist movement emerged at the beginning of the century but has not yet managed to wrench power from the white minority, literature is becoming very revolutionary in content, not only among the young writers of Soweto where members of cultural groups like the banned *Mudupe* used to read revolutionary poetry to the accompaniment of drums, rattles and flutes, but even among older, exiled writers like Dennis Brutus, the poet, and Alex La Guma, who was an active member of the South African Communist Party before he went into exile.

The issues raised in this chapter lead to one conclusion: that the dynamics of political struggles and social change affect the content and form of works of art, so that if we are to understand fully and appreciate the rise, development, concerns and styles of the literature of a nation we must see that literature in relation to the history and struggles of its people, and in relation to the various ideologies that issue from socio-economic conditions.

Notes

1 *Marxism and Literature*, p. 55.
2 See *On Socialist Ideology and Culture*, p. 20.
3 See Louis Althusser, *Lenin and Philosophy*, pp. 222–3.
4 See M. Lichtheim, *Ancient Egyptian Literature*, Vol. I, University of California Press, 1975.
5 R. Southall, *Literature, the Individual and Society*, p. 12.
6 Ibid., p. 15.
7 Lenin, *On Literature and Art*, p. 49.
8 *Studies in European Realism*, p. 212
9 Vázquez, *Art and Society*, pp. 116–17.
10 S. Mutswairo, *Feso*, Cape Town, Oxford University Press, 1957.
11 Vázquez, op. cit., p. 113.
12 See *Writer and Critic*, p. 64.
13 *Consciencism*, p. 57.
14 *The Wretched of the Earth*, p. 192.
15 Caudwell, *Studies and Further Studies in a Dying Culture*, p. 54.
16 See *The Historical Novel*, p. 301 ff.
17 Fanon, op. cit., p. 193.
18 The last verse of the song reads as follows:

Aya ndiwo mashoko
Akataurwa kare
Naivo Va Mao
Vachitidzidzisa

'These are the words
which Mao
Spoke long ago
In order to teach us'.

19 See Kadhani, M. and Zimunya, M. *And Now the Poets Speak*, p. 1.

4 The Rise and Development of the Modern African Novel – A Marxist Viewpoint

▼▼▼▼▼▼▼▼▼▼▼▼▼▼▼▼▼▼▼▼▼▼▼▼▼▼▼▼▼▼

Class, History and the African Novel

'The rise of a genre,' says David Craig, 'is likely to occur along with the rise of a class.'[1] This clearly applies to the rise of the novel in general, as was explained in the previous chapter, but it also has a special significance for the modern African novel. The African novel not only arose with the emergence of a class, but also at a time of violent social change. Craig's fourth law of literary development says 'such an emergence is likely to take place at a time of social upheaval.'[2]

The emerging class was the African intelligentsia, the product of colonial missionary education. Achebe, Camara Laye, Ngugi – all these were members of the rising African élite. The time of social upheaval was the time of agitation for independence. Nationalist movements were already clamouring for national independence and the colonial powers had come to accept the necessity of granting sovereignty to their former colonies, albeit without relinquishing their economic hold on these territories. Thus *Things Fall Apart* was first published in 1958, a year after the independence of Ghana, and two years later, in 1960, Nigeria assumed sovereign independence. Ngugi's first novel, *Weep Not, Child*, was published in 1964, the year when Kenya achieved independence. Meanwhile Mongo Beti published several novels between 1955 and 1958, including *The Poor Christ of Bomba*, published in 1956. An examination of the political and literary history of Africa will show that the period 1957–67 was not only a decade of intense political activity, a period when large numbers of African states agitated for and acquired independence, but was also a decade of lively artistic creativity when the African writer of English or French expression emerged as a force demanding world attention. But how do we account for this sudden burgeoning, this phenomenal upsurge of literary productivity? The explanation is not only that there was a new class of intellectuals emerging on the African social scene, but more importantly, that the new literary mood was an expression in artistic form of the rising political consciousness of the African people. Just as the emerging bourgeoisie was leading the political struggle, the emerging intelligentsia was expressing the new-found aspirations of the African people in the form of art.

There was a great deal of poetry written and also some drama. Poetry found successful expression in the négritude poets of the French-speaking world, notably Léopold Senghor and David Diop, while Soyinka became the leading playwright of Anglophone Africa. But the genre that flourished and placed itself on the world map was the novel, as evidenced by the achievements of Achebe, Camara Laye, Armah, Ngugi, Ousmane and others. These authors not only used the novel, which was the dominant popular form of the bourgeois world into which Africa had been hurled by history, but also utilized the genre which was most popular in their traditions, i.e. the legend. In African tradition, the legend was the centre of art and cultural life. The *griot* who recited the exploits of kings and of their ancestors was important in Africa,[3] but he was not as popular and widespread as the ordinary storyteller who, every evening in due season, held his audience spellbound by the charm of his narrative, giving pleasure to the listener and at the same time teaching the morals and beliefs of the community to the young. These stories which the young people listened to at home were later reinforced by the reading of literature at school and at university; and, naturally, the most accessible genre was the novel. This assertion is supported by the fact that even among those who wrote in African languages, the novel was the dominant form. In Lesotho, writers like Thomas Mofolo, the author of the historical novel *Chaka* had already appeared on the literary scene, while in Zimbabwe the works of Patrick Chakaipa, Emmanuel Ribeiro and Chidyausiku were fast replacing the traditional storyteller.

Mao Tse-Tung has said: 'In the world today all culture, all literature and art belong to definite classes and are geared to definite political lines. There is in fact, no such a thing as art for art's sake, art that stands above classes or art that is detached from or independent of politics.'[4] Nowhere is this truth more clearly demonstrated than in the form and content of the early African novel written in English or French. French and English were languages which could only be effectively used by the rising bourgeois-intellectual élite. Amos Tutuola who had little education is an exception, but the fact that he is an exception even shows itself in his style. Tutuola has even been accused of illiteracy by his more educated compatriots. In content, the novels reflected the socio-political activities and thinking of the time: the theme of culture contact and culture conflict; the story of the African young man who goes overseas to the metropolis and comes back to play a leading role in national life, as in the case of Camara in *The African Child* and Obi in *No Longer at Ease*; the theme of political agitation against the colonial powers as in Ngugi's early novels. With regard to culture contact and culture conflict, it is noteworthy that the educated African was the focus of the conflict. This is beautifully dramatized in the contradictions depicted in Achebe's novel *Arrow of God*, where Oduche, the mission-educated son of the Chief Priest, becomes the very symbol of the disintegration of the traditional religion of which the Chief Priest is the pillar.

These same mission-educated intellectuals, who were at one time so effectively colonized that they worshipped at the altar of colonial languages and culture and despised their own languages and way of life, were also destined to be the champions of intellectual decolonization at the time of Africa's re-awakening from the deep sleep of colonial domination. It was the bourgeois-intellectual élite, the intelligentsia, who came out with the négritude philosophy, the notion of the African personality and the drive to reassert the positive elements of African tradition which found expression in Camara Laye's *The African Child* and Achebe's two novels, *Things Fall Apart* and *Arrow of God*. No wonder, therefore, that the typical hero of the African novel of that time was a representative of this class – Camara in *The African Child*, Obi in *No Longer at Ease*, and Kamara in William Conton's *The African*. In other words, at this crisis point in African history, at the dawn of a new era in African political and social life, the African élite took it upon itself to challenge the dominant imperialist and colonial ideology of the time and to project the ideology of a rising national bourgeoisie. To this end Soyinka is quite right in characterizing négritude as 'the property of a bourgeois-intellectual élite.'[5]

It is significant that with only one exception, none of the early works of the realist novelists mentioned so far use representatives of the working class as protagonists, and that the only exception, Sembène Ousmane, was himself a proletarian. The majority of the early novelists writing in English and French not only reflected the interests of the emerging intelligentsia, but were also bourgeois in orientation. Their education was bourgeois in content and their lives were dominated by the values of western bourgeois society which had colonized and dominated Africa for over seventy years. However, their aim in writing was not to promote but to reject, at least in part, western political and cultural domination. Thus Camara Laye's autobiographical novel, *The African Child*, sentimentalizes and idealizes African tradition in an attempt to rebuff the European idea that Africans were savages and uncivilized before the coming of the white man. Achebe probably depicted the past of his ancestors more realistically in *Things Fall Apart* and *Arrow of God*, for in asserting the positive aspects of the African past, he did not conceal the dark side of the culture of the fathers of old. In *The River Between*, Ngugi not only voiced a rejection of colonialism, but also dramatized the contradiction between Christianity and traditional religion, while in Mongo Beti's *The Poor Christ of Bomba*, the contradictions in western Christianity were subjected to a severe critical and satirical examination. The political aspirations of the new African leaders and the agitation against colonialism were also reflected in the novels of T. M. Aluko, Peter Abrahams, Elechi Amadi, Ferdinand Oyono and other writers.[6]

Creative Writers, Scholars and Political Ideologists

To show that writing was not an isolated activity but an expression of the general political consciousness of the Africans at this stage, it is necessary to point out that while creative writers were producing novels, poems and plays nationalist leaders and academics were writing political and philosophical works. Thus, Kwame Nkrumah published *I Speak of Freedom: A Statement of*

African Ideology (Heinemann 1961), *Neo-Colonialism: The Last Stages of Imperialism* (Panaf 1965), *Consciencism: Philosophy and Ideology for Decolonisation* (1964, Monthly Review Press, 1970) and a number of other books. Ezekiel Mphahlele published *The African Image* (Faber 1962) and Albert Luthuli wrote his *Let My People Go* (McGraw-Hill 1962). Other leaders who produced political works include Léopold Senghor, Patrice Lumumba and Tom Mboya.[7] These ideologists of the nationalist movement were not only members of the emerging bourgeoisie, but many of them had a direct link with writers of fiction because, like the latter, they were drawn from the ranks of the intelligentsia. Mphahlele, who in *The African Image* wrote about the African personality, négritude and African nationalism, was also a creative writer.

One of the most influential political ideologists was a product of the African diaspora. Born in Martinique in 1925, Frantz Fanon eventually identified with the African cause in general and the Algerian revolution in particular, and was destined to exert considerable influence on African literary thought.[8] Significantly enough, Fanon was one of the first theoreticians to analyse négritude from a philosophical Marxist point of view. He saw négritude as a mark of the reawakening of the African from the clasp of cultural imperialism, an emotional reaction to Europe's contempt of the African and his cultural heritage.

> The concept of Negro-ism, for example, was the emotional if not the logical antithesis of that insult which the white man flung at humanity. This rush of Negro-ism against the white man's contempt showed itself in certain spheres to be the one idea capable of lifting interdictions and anathemas. Because the New Guinean or Kenyan intellectuals found themselves above all up against a general ostracism and delivered to the combined contempt of their over-lords, their reaction was to sing praises in admiration of each other. The unconditional affirmation of African culture has succeeded the unconditional affirmation of European culture.[9]

In more recent years, another political revolutionary, the late Amilcar Cabral of Guinea-Bissau, made pronouncements on another issue which is directly relevant to the present discussion, that of the relationship between politics and economic conditions on the one hand, and culture (therefore literature) on the other. According to Cabral, there are 'dependent and reciprocal relationships existing between the *cultural situation* and the *economic* (and political) *situation* in the behaviour of human societies.' Culture, he goes on, 'is always in the life of a society...the more or less conscious result of the economic and political activities of that society, the more or less direct expression of the kinds of relationships which prevail in that society.'[10] Cabral confirms the view expressed earlier in this chapter that the upsurge of literary activity in the fifties and sixties was an expression of a new political consciousness in Africa. The Marxist leader argues that culture plays a vital role on the ideological plane as an element of resistance to foreign domination, and further asserts that liberation struggles 'are preceded by an increase in expression of culture, consolidated progressively into a successful or unsuccessful attempt to affirm the cultural personality of the dominated people, as a means of negating the oppressor culture.'[11]

Another intellectual who influenced African thought in the drive against neo-colonialism and cultural imperialism is the Senegalese scholar, Cheikh Anta Diop who, according to the blurb on the back cover of *The African Origin of Civilization* 'shared with the later W. E. B. DuBois an award as the writer who had exerted the greatest influence on Negro thought in the 20th century.' One of Diop's basic arguments, that 'Ancient Egypt was a Negro civilization,' and that 'the history of Black Africa will remain suspended in air and cannot be written correctly until African historians dare to connect it with the history of Egypt'[12] finds full expression in Armah's historical novel, *Two Thousand Seasons*, whose very opening sentence, 'We are not a people of yesterday,' is a forceful and uncompromising rejection of the theory that Africa did not have a history of her own until she came into contact with Europe. As suggested in *Stylistic Criticism and the African Novel*, Armah believes that the original home of the African peoples is North Africa, meaning the area over which Ancient Egypt extended and the region now called the Sahara Desert. This is perfectly in line with and supportive of Diop's thesis that in the course of history Blacks left Egypt, penetrated deeper and deeper into the interior of the continent, and eventually lost touch with the motherland.[13]

What all this shows is that the writer was not an isolated seer. He was part and parcel of an intellectual mood sweeping the whole continent. It also shows that there was a great deal of cross-fertilization of ideas between creative writers and other intellectuals. The writings of committed novelists, political ideologists and talented academics were an expression, in ideological terms, of a new social psychology, a new level of political and ideological awareness after an era of acceptance of and submission to colonial domination, cultural imperialism and capitalist exploitation.

The African Writer and African Independence

By 1967 Ngugi felt that the African writer had failed.[14] The failure referred to here was in fact not that of the African writer alone. It resulted from the failure of the African bourgeoisie to give meaningful freedom and independence to the broad masses of the people. The African politician and the African writer had joined hands in the campaign against colonialism and cultural imperialism. This is in accordance with the general trend and laws of socio-political struggles. In times of social upheaval democratic forces, regardless of different class interests, often join hands to confront a common enemy in the national democratic revolution. But when the enemy is defeated the differences between groups and classes will reassert themselves so that the struggle takes on a new face. And so in less than a decade of their rule, many African leaders proved that they were incapable of shaking off the shackles of neo-colonialism, and joining hands with the international bourgeoisie to exploit the masses. The essence of Ngugi's complaint, therefore, was that by failing to challenge this new state of affairs, the African writer was guilty of neglecting his duty to society in general and to the African masses in particular.

Whereas the writer had joined the nationalists in challenging the ideology of the imperialists, it was now incumbent upon him to throw in his lot with the masses once more by confronting the ideology of the new ruling élite. A new rift had surfaced in independent Africa, not between Blacks and Whites, but between the haves and have-nots, what Ngugi has called 'a horizontal rift dividing the élite from the mass of the people.'[15] It was no longer sufficient to reject western notions about the African by singing lyrics about his past as Achebe and Camara Laye had done in *Things Fall Apart* and *The African Child*, for now 'conflicts between the emergent élitist middle-class and the masses were developing, their seeds being in the colonial pattern of social and economic development.'[16]

True to the mission of the writer in exploitative societies, the African writer responded by producing works that dealt a heavy blow to the ideology, aspiration and life-styles of the new ruling class. Significantly enough, one of the first authors to show his disaffection with the black rulers was Achebe, he who had sung praises to the culture of the fathers of old in protest against imperialist distortions of the African heritage. The stark reality of the new mode of exploitation resulted in *A Man of the People*, which, although it did not give an answer to the problem posed by the ruling African middle class, nevertheless managed to put the question by satirizing the class. One of the most significant novels of this period was Armah's *The Beautyful Ones Are Not Yet Born*. This powerful novel, the most devastating critique of post-independence corruption yet published, heralded the emergence of the revolutionary novel in Africa. Indeed two major socialist-inspired novels had already seen the light of day, Ousmane's *God's Bits of Wood* and Ngugi's *A Grain of Wheat*, but the former was a critique of the French colonial bourgeoisie, not of the African national bourgeoisie, while the latter's socialist content was so implicit that it could not be easily characterized as a socialist or revolutionary novel. It was during the next decade, during the 1970s that we were to witness the fire and ideological fervour of such novels as *Why Are We So Blest?* (1972), *Season of Anomy* (1973), *Two Thousand Seasons* (1973), *Petals of Blood* (1977) and Alex La Guma's *In the Fog of the Seasons' End* (1977). Talking of such novels which he describes as 'works of an assertive secular vision,' Soyinka has declared that they 'reveal the current trend in African writing, a trend which is likely to be more and more dominant as the intelligentsia of the continent seek ideological solutions that are truly divorced from the superstitious accretions of our alien encounters.'[17]

Ngugi expressed what he saw as the new trend in more clearly defined ideological terms than Wole Soyinka's words quoted above. By talking about the African past, Ngugi said, the writer had 'scorched the snake of colonialism, not killed it.'[18] Not everyone will agree with his conclusions, but as far as he was concerned there was now a younger generation of writers who were charting a new path, challenging the claims of the capitalist system inherited from the colonial past:

> To gain belief in ourselves that Achebe talks about, some of the younger African writers now realize not only that they must reclaim their past, but that the very condition of a successful and objective reclamation is the dismantling of all colonial institutions, and especially capitalism, as patterns of social and economic development.[19]

These views were expressed in his famous address entitled *The Writer and his Past.* In the same address he was bold enough to urge other writers to be committed on the side of the majority and to reject capitalism: 'It is only in a socialist context that a look at yesterday can be meaningful in illuminating today and tomorrow. Whatever his ideological persuasion, this is the African writer's task.'[20]

In the political arena, a new ideological awareness was beginning to dawn on some of the statesmen and, in particular, on leaders of nationalist movements still fighting for independence. In 1968 Juluis Nyerere, the great statesman of Africa, published his *Ujamaa: Essays on Socialism* in which he rejects the capitalist mode of production in favour of his 'African Socialism.' Such publications mark a more profound and deeper understanding of the meaning and implications of independence than was prevalent in the 1950s and early sixties. The question now was not just 'independence' but 'what form of independence?' This was the question posed by those countries which gained their freedom through protracted armed struggles in the seventies and eighties – Mozambique, Angola, Guinea-Bissau and Zimbabwe. When they acquired their freedom, these countries had a different concept of independence from the countries which had acceded to sovereignty in the previous two decades. Their long struggle for independence, and the experience of independent African countries now under the grip of neo-colonialism taught them to look at national independence from a radical ideological point of view, and they consequently chose the socialist path to development.

The Role of Productive Forces – Conclusion

It would be quite wrong to advance a theory of literary development which does not take into account the role of productive forces and the level of material production. The introduction of capitalism in Africa by the colonial powers brought about a technological transformation of the continent and this had a bearing on literary production. It has been said that the artistic modes of production possessed by a society are 'a crucial factor in determining . . . the very literary form of the work itself.'[21] The availability of the printing press and the printed word was a contributing factor in the development of modern African literature. Whereas the illiterate society of Africa's communal and feudal past relied on the storyteller for moral instruction and on the fable and the song for aesthetic pleasure, the emerging bourgeois society could now capitalize on new means of artistic production and on their ability to read and write. Indeed we can ask with Karl Marx, 'Is it not inevitable that with the emergence of the press bar the singing and the telling the muse cease?'[22]

Furthermore, the fable was no longer an adequate medium for voicing the aspirations of the new society created by the changing socio-political conditions, for while the general tenor of the fable was to reinforce the traditional mores, there was now a need not only to mirror a changing society, but also to voice the discontent of a people suffering under the yoke of foreign domination, to herald in artistic form the dawn of a new epoch. As a result of these technological, ideological and economic developments, traditional modes of literature were quickly submerged and supplanted by the novel and by modern poetry and drama.

The argument advanced here is that the African novel is not only the product of a class – the intelligentsia – but also the result of historical conditions. Modern African literature should not be seen in isolation from the prevailing economic and socio-political conditions and from the dominant ideologies of the world in which it is produced. Equally important is the need to study African literature in its historical and intellectual context. To strip the African novel of historicity is to sink into empty and sterile academicism.

Notes

1 See David Craig (ed.) *Marxists on Literature*, p. 160.
2 Ibid., p. 160.
3 For the role of the *griot* in West African society see D. T. Niane, *Sundiata: An Epic of Old Mali*.
4 'Talks at the Yenan Forum on Literature and Art,' *Selected Works of Mao Tse-Tung*, Vol. 3, p. 86.
5 *Myth, Literature and the African World*, p. 135.
6 For a brief guide to the works of African writers see Zell and Silver (eds.) *A Reader's Guide to African Literature*.
7 A brief account of the non-fiction literature of the time is given in Zell and Silver, *A Reader's Guide to African Literature*.
8 Fanon's influence can be felt in the works of Armah and Ngugi. For his influence on Armah, see Robert Fraser, *The Novels of Ayi Kwei Armah*, pp. 7–10.
9 *The Wretched of the Earth*, p. 171.
10 *Return to Source: Selected Speeches of Amilcar Cabral*, p. 41.
11 Ibid., p. 43.
12 *The African Origin of Civilization: Myth or Reality*, p. xiv.
13 Ibid., pp. 22–3.

14 Zell and Silver, op. cit., pp. 157–8.
15 See *Homecoming*, p. 24.
16 Ibid., pp. 44–5.
17 *Myth, Literature and the African World*, p. 87.
18 See *Homecoming*, p. 45.
19 Ibid., p. 45.
20 Ibid., p. 46.
21 Eagleton, *Marxism and Literary Criticism*, pp. 67–8.
22 See Marx and Engels, *On Literature and Art*, p. 84.

5 *Ideology and Language in African Literature*

▼▼▼▼▼▼▼▼▼▼▼▼▼▼▼▼▼▼▼▼▼▼▼▼▼▼▼▼▼▼▼

The Language Situation in Africa

Before we open the discussion on the language situation in Africa, it is necessary to reiterate two observations made in the previous chapter: first, that African literature is the product of a bourgeois intellectual élite brought up on a diet of western education; and secondly, that African literature should be seen in its historical context. These observations are important in our discussion of the language of African writers.

The African bourgeois intellectual élite was not only given a western education, but also taught in western European languages to the extent that education was equated with the acquisition of a European language. Education and all official business was conducted in a European language while African languages, many of which were not codified, were relegated to the home and other informal situations. A research project carried out by the present writer in Zimbabwe before it achieved independence indicated that Shona-English bilinguals used English even for such purposes as writing friendly letters, while Shona, their mother tongue, was restricted to the home and other informal situations.[1]

An important feature of African history is that when the continent emerged from colonialism it found itself in the anomalous situation of having to continue using colonial languages as official languages, for education, technological and cultural development and international communication. There are a number of reasons for this. In the first place, no African language was sufficiently developed to be used for all the needs of a modern state. Secondly, most African nations are multilingual states where each indigenous language is only spoken by a section of the population in a particular region. It is also evident that for any developing country to achieve a measure of technological and economic development it needs access to the outside world; it needs the assistance of more developed countries, and this necessitates the use of a world language like English or French. Lastly, the attempt to unite the nations and peoples of Africa which resulted in the formation of the Organization of African Unity gave rise to the need for an international language, and as there was no Pan-African language which could be adopted by all the nations of Africa, French, English and Arabic were retained for the purpose.

Since independence there has been an attempt to develop and enhance African languages, but with the exception of Swahili in Tanzania and Amharic in Ethiopia, these languages have remained subordinate to European ones. There has also been a general attempt to revive African culture, but much of the work done in this sphere is conducted in a European language.

In this situation, it was not surprising that the majority of outstanding African writers, who also belonged to the educated élite, chose to write in a European language, although some wrote in their mother tongue. Among those who chose to write in their own language are D. O. Fagunwa, the Yoruba novelist, Thomas Mofolo of Lesotho and the Zimbabwean novelist, Patrick Chakaipa. In a number of countries, such as Zimbabwe and Lesotho, the majority of writers use African languages. But what is significant in the development of African literature is that those who write in a European language have completely over-shadowed those who write in their mother tongue. One reason for this is that writers like Achebe, Armah, Ngugi and others appeal to an international reader-ship which gives their work a great deal of publicity. In fact, African writers using French and English originally wrote with a western audience in mind. As Hamidou Kane once put it, 'The African writers, with a beneficial sense of opportunism, decided to direct their action mainly towards Europe and the world outside Africa.'[2] And he adds, 'The very nature of our literature, the conditions governing its birth and development are such that there is no choice.'[3]

Kane here highlights the Eurocentricism of the African writer which he shares with the African politician and the African scholar, a fact that has a direct bearing on the problem of neo-colonialism discussed below.

The Implications of Writing in European Languages – Ngugi's Position

The use of colonial languages to write African literature has given rise to a number of questions, some ideological and some relating to the definition and criticism of African literature. The problem was first brought to the fore by Obiajunwa Wali in the 1960s when he raised the whole question as to whether literature written in a European language could be classified as African, and went on to declare that to be truly African, African literature 'must be written in African languages'.[4] The present writer has discussed these issues elsewhere.[5] Here we are concerned with the ideological implications of the problem, with such issues as cultural imperialism, neo-colonialism and the relationship between the writer and his audience. These problems have been most forcefully articulated by Ngugi wa Thiong'o, one of the leading writers in English.[6]

For Ngugi, a foreign language cannot correctly reflect the historical con-sciousness of a people. Since it is a process of thinking in images, the literature of a people draws upon their collective experience; in other words, upon their history, which is embodied in their language. It is therefore imperative for

Kenyan writers to ask: 'Whose language and history will our literature draw upon? Foreign languages and the history and cultures carried by those languages? Or national languages ... and the histories and cultures carried by those languages?'[7] According to Ngugi, it therefore follows that literature written in a European language reflects the historical consciousness of the foreigners. In colonial Kenya, English was taught to safeguard European interests and to promote British bourgeois culture, since 'at the same time as the English language was being encouraged and the British bourgeois culture carried by that language was being promoted, Kenyan national languages were being actively suppressed'.[8] Here, Ngugi goes to the root of cultural imperialism and proceeds to argue that by continuing to write in a European language African writers are in fact participating in the consolidation of neo-colonialism in Africa. One of the most successful users of a European language in Africa, he is now of the opinion that the body of literature produced by Africans in English, French and Portuguese is not African literature at all, but *Afro-European literature*.[9] Ngugi has decided to live up to this declaration by writing in Gikuyu, although his books are inevitably translated into English. An example of this is the novel *Caitaani Mutharaba-ini* which has been published in English as *Devil on the Cross*.

Ngugi also discusses the issue raised by Hamidou Kane in 1966: the all-important question of the audience. For Ngugi, to choose a language is to choose a world, as this inevitably leads to the question: 'For whom do I write? Who is my audience?' If a Kenyan writer writes in English 'he cannot possibly reach or directly talk to the peasants and workers of Kenya.'[10] Mohamadou Kane expressed the problem most succinctly when he criticized the rupture between the African writer and the African public by drawing the following analogy: 'In actual fact, our writing is like Soviet industry before Khrushchev, concerned only with production, the consumer being forced to do everything else'. And he adds, 'You must agree the situation of African writers is rather special in that they want to be representatives of a people whose aspirations they do not always worry about.'[11] This is a heavy indictment on the African writer, showing a major contradiction between his anti-imperialist stance on the one hand and the class with which he aligns himself on the other.

By writing in a language which the broad masses can neither speak nor understand, the African writer alienates himself from the people and appears to align himself at best with his own class, the African intellectual élite, and at worst with his colonialist masters. The implications of this merit further consideration.

European Languages and the Fight Against Cultural Imperialism

Ngugi describes language as the memory-bank of a people and an embodiment of both continuity and change in the historical consciousness of a people. For the purpose of our argument, what needs to be emphasized is that linguistic studies in modern times have shown that each language reflects the concerns, attitudes and assumptions of its speakers. The present writer has pointed out elsewhere that the use of a language carries with it the prejudices, habits and mannerisms of its native speakers.[12] Foreign speakers of a language find themselves willy-nilly projecting the views of the native speakers. There is, for instance, a fairly large number of 'loaded words' in any language, words whose pejorative and ameliorative connotations arise from the social psychology of the native speaker, from the store of prejudices, opinions and value judgements which form an important part of his culture, from the native speaker's image of himself as a member of a dearly beloved race, and from his image of other not-so-dearly beloved races. When the language in question is a colonial language like English or French, those who learn it as a second language find themselves sharing the native speaker's world view; they will see themselves and the native speaker through the latter's eyes. Examples of such loaded words in English are 'native', 'savage', 'primitive', 'pagan', 'witchdoctor', which were commonly on the lips of British people during the colonial era and constituted an important element of the vocabulary passed on to those African 'natives' who had the good fortune of learning the 'civilized language' of the British. These words referred to the conquered races, not to the conquerors. African rulers and ethnic groups were referred to as 'chiefs', 'tribes', and 'war-like natives', whereas European rulers and their soldiers were described in such terms as 'Their Imperial Majesties', 'the Emperor', 'potentates', 'princess' and 'warriors.'

Language also has a class character. Bernstein's socio-linguistic studies have made educationists and linguists sharply aware of language varieties and, in particular, of the differences between standard varieties and non-standard varieties. Bernstein's thesis is based on the relationship between language and class, i.e. on the idea that social class produces a certain type of language while language use reinforces social class. The theory rests on the concept of the 'elaborated code' and the 'restricted code'. These terms refer to two types of speech – one which is more versatile and explicit (the elaborated code) and another which is more restricted and less explicit (the restricted code). These codes have a class basis and have the effect of reinforcing social differentiation. While all people have access to the restricted code (which is inferior) not all people have access to the elaborated code (which is superior). Bernstein associates the former with the British working class and the latter with the British middle class. 'It is considered that the normative systems associated with the middle class and associated strata are likely to give rise to modes of an elaborated code whilst those associated with some sections of the working class are likely to create individuals limited to a restricted code.'[13]

The important point from Bernstein's thesis is that British working-class people were seen to be 'linguistically deprived', leading to poor academic performance. The result was that in Britain and America attempts were made to alleviate the problems of working-class children by adapting them to middle-class norms of speech and behaviour.

In other words, it was believed that working-class children suffered from verbal deprivation by virtue of belonging to their class, and that the way to solve their problem was to teach them middle-class modes of speech, i.e. to help them to acquire Standard English. The important lesson here is that British Standard English, American Standard English and the varieties that were exported to the colonies reflected the culture, prejudices and world views of the middle and upper classes of Britain and America. In other words, when we talk of British cultural imperialism we are in fact talking about the projection through the English language and other institutions of the ideology of the ruling classes in Britain, i.e. the bourgeoisie and the aristocracy. The aim of cultural imperialism was not only to undermine the culture of the colonized peoples, but also to create, through the education system, an African élite which cherished and promoted the bourgeois values that colonial languages and other instruments of cultural domination fostered. The use of a colonial language by African writers could therefore mean a promotion in independent Africa of western bourgeois values and world views, which in essence means the perpetuation of cultural imperialism and neo-colonialism, as Ngugi has argued.

At this juncture it is pertinent to pose two questions: first, does the use of an African language in itself necessarily lead to the end of western cultural domination? Second, can an African writer continue to use a European language and at the same time combat cultural imperialism?

In answering the first question it is important to admit that the use of African languages by African writers would be a very effective way of combating Eurocentricism and western cultural domination. But we must hasten to add that writing in African languages alone is not enough. With the advent of colonialism in Africa, European and African languages assumed a dominant-subordinate relationship with each other. A *dominant* language is one that is given a commanding position by the state, while a *subordinate* language is one that is given an inferior status. In colonial situations the language of the con-quering race is almost inevitably accorded a dominant position, while that of the subject race is given a subordinate role. In my study of the mutual impact of a European language and an African language I have shown how the former, as the dominant language, can have a profound effect on the vocabulary, syntax and phonology of the latter.[14] The influence goes so far as to affect the speaker's performance in his mother tongue. African speakers of English tend to be poor speakers of African languages and are characterized by the process called *code-switching*, whereby the native speaker of the subordinate language can hardly sustain a conversation in his own language and is compelled to use large chunks of English every now and then, a problem that does not arise when he is speaking English. Because African education is conducted in European languages, we assume the psychology and attitudes dictated by those languages even when we are speaking our own languages. What this means is that the influence of a dominant language on a subordinate one is a reflection of the impact of the culture of the ruling race which gradually erodes and replaces that of a subject race, even in the way the colonized people think and use their language.

It becomes obvious, therefore, that the mere fact of writing in African languages is not enough as a method of combating neo-colonialism and cultural imperialism. The need, first and foremost, is a high level of conscientization and an understanding of how cultural imperialism operates in both the colonial language and African languages. Without this, African writers could easily translate concepts expressed in English into African languages and end up dishing out chunks of neo-colonial culture to the masses in the masses' own idiom.

This brings us to the second question: whether African writers can continue to use European languages and at the same time combat cultural imperialism. The answer is certainly in the affirmative, though it is necessary to add that in order to combat cultural imperialism most effectively it would be ideal to use an African language. But this is a question we can come back to later. The point at issue is that if a language can be used as an instrument of colonial domination it can by the same token be used to combat colonialism. To understand this, it is important to be aware of the dialectical relationship that exists between language as a linguistic system and the individual as a user of that system. Language to some extent determines the way an individual sees reality by presenting reality to him as it is viewed by society, i.e. by the collective wisdom of the speakers of that language. But an individual can also help to shape the development of a language, be it his mother tongue or not. As Raymond Williams has commented, language, as a social phenomenon, 'must have an effective nucleus of meaning but in practice it has a variable range, corresponding to the endless variety of situations within which it is actively used'.[15] Depending on the situation, the individual can exploit this 'variable range' of language and add new shades of meaning to words by substituting pejorative connotations for pleasant ones or vice-versa. Because language is such a malleable tool, African writers have successfully used colonial languages like English and French to reject western imperialist ideology and to depict African culture in a favourable light. Armah, Achebe, Okara, Okot p'Bitek and to some extent the négritude poets have all managed in various ways and with varying degrees of success to portray Africans in a positive light and Europeans in a negative light, through the medium of English and French. In Armah's *Two Thousand Seasons*, for example, Europeans are 'destroyers' and Africans 'the people of the way'. The colour of white is associated with ugliness and death, while black is associated with the qualities of beauty and life. The 'black is beautiful' and 'white is ugly' theme is evident in Armah's description of White and Black characters. For example, white carries negative connotations in the following description of Bentum's White woman who is portrayed as a ghost:

Now from the gate to the falling came first an apparition exactly like a ghost: a pale white woman in white clothes moving with a disjointed, severe, jerky walk, like a profoundly discontented walker. Her walk was like that of a beginning stiltwalker, but an angry beginner. Her face was squeezed in a severe frown that had formed three permanent vertical creases on her lower forehead in the space between her eyes. She had no eyebrows. Eyelashes she had, but they were hard to discern, being white and therefore merging into the pallor of her face. On her head she wore a white hat. As she came in there was space before her, space to her left and right, space behind her: her figure seemed the shape itself of loneliness. It seemed impossible that she could ever be together with any other being.[16]

Now contrast the ugliness of this 'white phantom' with the beauty of Idawa, a black woman:

There was a woman. Idawa was her name. There are not many born with every generation of whom it may be said they have a beauty needing no counterpointing blemish to make its wonder clear. The best moulded face may lead the admiring eye in the end down to a pair of lumpen legs. The slenderest neck may sit incongruous on a bloated bosom. Idawa had a beauty with no such disappointment in it. Seen from a distance her shape in motion told the looker here was co-ordination free, unforced. From the hair on her head to the last of her toes there was nothing wasted in her shaping. And her colour: that must have come uninterfered with from night's own blackness.[17]

To appreciate Armah's unconventional use of English words we must remember that white has been traditionally associated with good values among the English and other European races, and black with everything bad and ugly. Sins are black and Satan is black, while virginity, purity and innocence are associated with white. In the Shona language the word used for 'sins' in some Christian churches is *zvitema*, 'the black things', a word which shows how the ideological content of European languages can be easily transferred to African languages.

An example from literature which illustrates our discussion of Armah's anti-colonial use of English words is the poem *The little Black Boy*, by the English poet, William Blake. In this poem Blake depicts a Black boy feeling guilty for being black and hoping to be white like an English child when he is in heaven. The little English boy, who is White, is likened to an angel, while the Black boy associates his black colour with darkness and absence of light. The Black boy says with great grief:

> My mother bore me in the southern wild,
> And I am black, but O! my soul is white;
> White as an angel is the English child,
> But I am black, as if bereav'd of light.
>
> *William Blake*

What Armah has done, therefore, is to use the English language to reject these racist assumptions by assuming a form of racialism in reverse. The advantage of doing this in the colonial language is that the colonial master himself can experience the shock of seeing this new image of himself, an image which corresponds to his own subjective image of the colonized peoples. It is an effective slap in the face of cultural imperialism. On the other hand, African peasants and workers who cannot read the language are unaffected by the message, and this is a major ideological contradiction to which we shall immediately turn.

African Literature and the African Masses

Talking of the inability of the modern western artist to communicate with the broad masses of the people, Vázquez has said, 'A profound manifestation of the hostility of capitalism to art is the fact that in bourgeois society the artist is necessarily divorced from the masses because he cannot descend to their level, and the masses do not want to raise themselves – nor can they – to the level of art; artists today cannot hope to share their art with the millions of human beings kept by capitalism in a reified state'.[18] On the other hand, art should not be the exclusive property of a minority because 'art is one of the most rewarding means which human beings (not just artists) possess to deepen their humanity'.[19]

The limitations on the relationship between artist and public may result from the principle of private property and from the language employed by the artist or the inability of the public to understand that language. Whereas in the context of the West Vázquez may be using the term *language* metaphorically to refer to the exclusive idiom or symbols employed by the artist, in Africa the statement can be interpreted literally. The broad masses of Africa are estranged from African literature by the writer's choice of a foreign language. Obviously, this imposes a severe limitation on the social function of literature, for literature has a social function and is seen by African writers to have one, since the African writer is committed. Authors like Achebe, Armah, Ngugi, La Guma, Sembène Ousmane and others took up the pen to participate in Africa's struggle against colonialism, cultural imperialism and the exploitation of man by man.

To fulfil its social function adequately, literature must be able to speak to the widest spectrum of society possible; it must be truly popular. It must be at once national and universal. It must reach the masses of the people in the writer's society and at the same time speak to universal man. Popular art depicts people in an historical moment, in the process of making history. In Africa and other developing nations, peasants, workers and the intelligentsia are actively involved in the process of making history. In Africa's struggle for independence, peasants and workers were fully mobilized and became an indispensable component of the political movements that were generally spearheaded by the petty-bourgeoisie and the intelligentsia. African writers are fully aware of this because their novels talk about peasants, workers and the educated élite, but their choice of language is such that they can only speak to the intelligentsia and are unable to communicate with the vast majority of the people.

One of the consequences of the breakdown in communication between the African writer and the African masses is that African literature in European languages cannot be classified as truly popular art. It should be understood here that by popular art we do not mean 'mass art' or impoverished low-level art produced with the idea of feeding the masses on such cheap stuff as detective stories, sensational romantic fiction, exciting adventure film stories or low-level pop music. As explained in the previous paragraph, the appeal of true popular art cuts across social classes. Popular art is capable of appealing to the highly educated while at the same time being intelligible to the common man. In the words of Bertolt Brecht, ' "Popular" means intelligible to the broad masses, taking over their own forms of expression and enriching them/adopting and consolidating their standpoint'. It also means 'intelligible to other sections too/linking with tradition and carrying it further/handing on the achievements of the section now leading to the section of the people that is struggling for the lead'.[20] Examples of popular works in this sense include the novels of Maxim Gorky and Mikhail Sholokhov which talk about the common man in ordinary language, but are capable of appealing to the most sophisticated reader. The works of, say, Achebe and Ousmane would doubtless speak to the people easily if they were written in the language of the masses, but alas, the broad masses of West Africa have no access to this literature which is written in a foreign idiom and speaks *about* them without speaking *to* them.

It is perhaps this contradiction between the social function of art and the estrangement of the public from it that has compelled Ngugi wa Thiong'o to write in his mother tongue, Gikuyu. By ensuring that his writings are subsequently translated into English, Ngugi goes some way towards resolving the problem of serving both the Kenyan masses and the international community. It would be ideal to have an African language that has acquired the status of an international language, but in the absence of such a language Ngugi's new approach seems to be one practical way of resolving the problem of the contradiction between the ideology of the writer and his chosen tongue.

Notes

1 See Ngara, *Bilingualism, Language Contact and Language Planning*, pp. 20–6.
2 See Hamidou Kane, 'The African Writer and his Public', in G. D. Killam, *African Writers on African Writing*, p. 55.
3 Ibid., p. 55
4 Wali, 'The Dead End of African Literature?' *Transition*, Vol. 3, No. 10.
5 See Ngara, *Stylistic Criticism and the African Novel*, Chapter 1.
6 See Ngugi wa Thiong'o, *Writers in Politics*, Chapter 5.
7 Ibid., p. 60
8 Ibid., p. 63.
9 Ibid., p. 59.
10 Ibid., p. 54.

11 See Kane, op. cit., p. 65.
12 See Ngara, 'A Redefinition of the Role of the English Language in African Universities,' *Bulletin of the Association of African Universities*, Vol. 1, No. 2, pp. 35–42.
13 B. Bernstein, *Class, Code and Control*, Vol. 1, p. 135.
14 See Ngara, *Bilingualism, Language Contact and Language Planning*, Chapters 8 and 9.
15 Raymond Williams, *Marxism and Literature*, p. 39.
16 Armah, *Two Thousand Seasons*, p. 119.
17 Ibid., pp. 69–70.
18 See A. S. Vásquez, *Art and Society*, p. 260.
19 Ibid., p. 238.
20 See Brecht, '*The Popular and the Realistic*', in D. Craig (ed.) *Marxists On Literature*, p. 423.

PART TWO
Studies in the Art and Ideology
of the African Novel

6 Ideology and Socialism in Three African Writers

▼▼▼▼▼▼▼▼▼▼▼▼▼▼▼▼▼▼▼▼▼▼▼▼▼▼

Introduction

The influence of Marxism on African writing cannot be restricted to those writers who have openly declared their commitment to socialism. There are other writers who to a greater or lesser degree have been influenced by the proliferation of Marxist ideas, whether consciously or unconsciously. In this connection it is important to point out that the influence of any ideology on a body of literature is largely a result of historical conditions and can enter unobtrusively into a writer's consciousness and creative work. Talking of the impact of the new conception of history on literature after the 1848 revolution in Europe, Georg Lukács has said: 'However it is not this philologically demonstrable influence which is important, but rather the *common character of the reactions to reality* which in history and literature produce analogous subjects and forms of historical consciousness.'[1] In the same way it can be said that the influence of socialist ideas on African writing may not be concretely and systematically demonstrable, but that the spreading of socialism in Africa and the world coupled with the disenchantment of the African people with their new African leaders and the prolonged liberation struggles in some parts of the continent created suitable conditions for the diffusion of Marxist ideas in African writing. A proliferation of socialist ideas can be felt in Soyinka's *Season of Anomy*, in Festus Iyayi's *Violence* and in Sahle Selassie's third novel, *Firebrands*.[2] The contradictions between exploitative capitalism and progressive communalism as presented in *Season of Anomy* are explained in detail in *Stylistic Criticism and the African Novel* and we need not repeat the analysis here. This chapter is restricted to an explanation of socialist influences in three authors: Armah, Maillu and the early Ngugi. One of these, Ngugi wa Thiong'o, shows no clear inclination to socialism in his earliest writings but he has become more and more committed to its ideals in recent years.

The purpose of the chapter is to show how far the particular writer in the works under discussion is socialist orientated and to explain the ideology that issues from his works vis-à-vis socialist art. The analysis will therefore be a limited one being concerned mainly with ideological content, and will not be as comprehensive as in the rest of Part Two where the principles of Marxist stylistic criticism are applied in full.

Ayi Kwei Armah and the Drive Against Neo-Colonialism

No study of ideology in the African novel would be complete without a reference to Armah whose revolutionary writings have had a very strong ideological fervour from the time of his first novel, *The Beautyful Ones Are Not Yet Born*. Armah can easily be labelled 'Marxist' because of his militancy and it is necessary to determine what Marxist influences there are in his writings. Such influences are clearly discernible in *Two Thousand Seasons*,[3] and it is to this novel that we shall immediately turn.

Two Thousand Seasons is concerned with the assertion of African values and the rejection of foreign domination, foreign values and foreign social systems. This epic novel urges Africans to go back to their roots and discover their common origin. It urges them to find the 'way' which has been lost largely as a result of foreign influence. In pursuit of this aim, the book advocates a complete rejection of Christianity and Islam, a total condemnation of all things western and Arab, and a glorification of that which makes Africans noble, and that which promotes African unity. The background to this unusual vehemence – the racism of other racial groups and the Eurocentric ethnology of the times – has been fully and expertly explained by Wole Soyinka.[4] Soyinka maintains that *Two Thousand Seasons* 'is not a racist tract', with the emphasis on 'tract' because, as the eminent scholar proceeds to explain, 'the central theme is far too positive and dedicated'.[5]

There are many ideas and passages in this book which show that Armah is not only a progressive and positive thinker, but also upholds certain ideals which are consonant with the principles of socialism. There is a rejection of the monarchy and of feudal relations and practices. For instance, the author asserts the common ownership of land by attacking one king's attempt to seize the land: 'For the first time among us one man tried to turn land into something cut apart and owned' (p. 64). According to *Two Thousand Seasons* the whole idea of a class society, of the division between the ruler and the ruled, was externally imposed (p. 34 ff). Armah thus condemns class society and the rise of 'producers' or workers and 'parasites' or capitalists (p. 58). Towards the end of the book, there is an acceptance of guerrilla warfare or the armed struggle as the most effective method of ending Africa's political ills, a method which is characteristically communist. What is more, the last paragraph of the book is a most passionate articulation of the principle of revolutionary internationalism which rises above the confines of nationalism.

> Against this what a vision of creation yet unknown, higher, much more profound than all erstwhile creation! What a hearing of the confluence of all the waters of life flowing to overwhelm the ashen desert's blight! What an utterance of the coming together of all the people of our way, the coming together of all people of the way. (p. 206)

It is a powerful ending which shows that by the time he put down his pen, Armah had come to a recognition of the fact that the people of the way could not be restricted to Africa alone, that Africa's struggle is not an isolated one, but is part and parcel of an international struggle for freedom, social justice and equality.

Another way in which Armah's views are akin to Marxism is his materialist conception of religion which is evident in both *Two Thousand Seasons* and *The Healers*. The former novel is in design and style an epic, but unlike traditional epics it has no place for gods in its scheme of things. The people of the way are depicted – rather unrealistically – as a people without a god to guide their destiny. In *The Healers*, the author satirizes the superstitious beliefs of the Asante people of Ghana who offer human sacrifices to the spirits and commit all manner of atrocities in the hope of defeating the White man's gun by spiritual means. Here we witness how superstitious mysticism attempts to fight technology to no avail.[6]

Finally, three of Armah's novels promote the principle of egalitarianism in African society. In *Why Are We So Blest?* Solo is an advocate of egalitarianism and is disappointed by the inequalities he finds so glaringly manifest in his host country – obviously Algeria – which he thought had done away with privileges.[7] Of *Two Thousand Seasons* Soyinka has said, 'Ayi Kwei Armah asserts a past whose social philosophy was a natural egalitarianism, unravelling events which produced later accretions of the materialist ethic in order to reinforce the unnaturalness, the abnormalities of the latter'.[8] In *The Healers* there is hope not only for a united Africa, but also for a society without kings or slaves, a society in which there are no social divisions, where people regard each other simply as 'people. Human beings who respect each other' (p. 214).

In other respects, however, Armah's philosophy goes counter to some of the basic principles of Marxism. This is true of the strong racial element in *Two Thousand Seasons*. Whereas Marxist philosophy sees the struggle for justice and equality in terms of class, Armah sees the African predicament from the point of view of race. The antagonisms in *Two Thousand Seasons* are expressed in terms of 'White' versus 'Black', Arabs and Europeans versus Africans. And although the book presents a critique of monarchism and oppression, the struggle against monarchist rule is not presented from a proletarian or peasant point of view. The emergence of class society is denigrated, but the nature of the class society and the class struggle is not clear. There is no question of embracing the Marxist concept of the class struggle here for 'whatever goes against the white destroyers' empire, that thing alone is beautiful, that consciousness alone has satisfaction for the still living mind' (p. 205–6). In actual fact Marxism is rejected in *Why Are We So Blest?* as 'the whitest of philosophies' (p. 163). And realism, in the sense of 'typical characters under typical circumstances' is violated in both *Two Thousand Seasons* and *The Healers*, because both books are constructed upon a mythical past and do not have realistic characters like Achebe's Okonkwo or Ezeulu.

If he consciously rejects Marxism, wherein then lies Armah's revolutionary ideology? In my opinion Armah is basically a fervent nationalist whose ideology rests on two principles: vehement anti-neo-colonialism and passionate Pan-Africanism. In this he seems to have been influenced by Frantz Fanon and to some extent by Cheikh Anta Diop. The attack on neo-colonialism runs through nearly all of Armah's novels. *The Beautyful Ones Are Not Yet Born* is not directed against imperialism and neo-colonialism as such. The main emphasis here is to expose the fallacy and emptiness of African independence and the pervasive corruption that the author observed in Nkrumah's Ghana. But even here Armah spares no effort to lash out at the ugly head of neo-colonialism which takes the form of what he symbolically calls 'the gleam', i.e. the yearning for things European by the rising bourgeoisie who look down upon their own African way of life and hanker after western bourgeois luxuries and life-styles.

It is in *Why Are We So Blest?* that neo-colonialism is defined in precise terms, for here Armah has discovered the imperialist machinations behind the African disease exposed in *The Beautyful Ones*. The chief protagonists in this new novel are Modin Dofu, a Ghanaian who starts off as a student in America and eventually attempts to join a liberation movement operating from a North African country, evidently Algeria; Solo, a failed writer from a Portuguese colony in Africa; and Aimee, a White American girl who has a love affair with Modin.

When he gets to America, Modin discovers that the African is stereotyped as an unintelligent, sub-human creature. Those like him who manage to get into American universities are said to be exceptions to the rule. And western education itself, Modin realizes, is élitist and designed to alienate the educated African from his people and to bring him into alliance with imperialism so as to subjugate the masses more effectively. European education, like all other institutions, is aimed at blindfolding the African: 'all the institutions set up by the Europeans are traps to destroy awareness' (p. 223). These institutions are backed by a powerful propaganda machinery which props up the so-called development projects:

She gave me some magazines to read. She said: 'Here's some of the propaganda.'
I was a bit confused. The magazines were about development projects in Africa, the West Indies, New Guinea, and some places in America. In each of them black people were being helped by white people. (pp. 108–9)

For their part, African leaders seek to ape their former colonial masters, doing no more than step into their masters' shoes rather than change things for the better. Hence, 'The guide told us it was extremely important for the President to live exactly where the British governor had lived' (p. 76). This aping of the White man is symptomatic of a worse disease – the dependence of African governments on western powers and their consequent neglect and betrayal of the African masses: 'The main political characteristic of African leadership since the European invasion is its inability and unwillingness to connect organically with the African people because it always wants first of all to connect with Europe and Europeans' (p. 221).

Armah's observations here seem to be directly influenced by Fanon who, incidentally, is mentioned by name on page 48 of the same novel. Not only did Fanon criticize the neglect of the masses by the bourgeoisie in Africa and the Third World at large, but he condemned in the strongest terms the dependence of the African bourgeoisie, and therefore of independent African states, on Europe, a dependence which inevitably leads to dangerous economic control. This, to Fanon, is typical of neo-colonial relations:

> The economic channels of the young state sink back inevitably into neo-colonialist lines. The national economy, formerly protected, is today literally controlled. The budget is balanced through loans and gifts, while every three or four months the chief ministers themselves or else their governmental delegations come to the erstwhile mother countries or elsewhere, fishing for capital.[9]

The relationship between Africa and Europe is symbolized in the love affair between Modin and Aimee and the imagined sexual contact between Aimee and Mwangi. Both lead to destruction. Modin's love affair with Aimee leads to his death, as in the same way Aimee sees her husband aiming a gun at the head of the 'primitive' African house boy whom she has, to all intents and purposes, forced to submit to her sexual desires (pp. 186–9). The relationship between Aimee and Mwangi corresponds with the colonial period, when Europe forced 'primitive Africa' into colonial subservience and exploitation whereas the mutual agreement between Aimee and Modin corresponds to the post-independence neo-colonialist relationship between the West and Africa. In both cases it is the European who benefits and the African who suffers.

The frustrated writer, Solo, can see the dangers of Africa's flirtation with Europe much more clearly than Modin. He is able to see the relationship between Modin and Aimee as that of 'the African absorbed into Europe, trying to escape death, eager to shed privilege, not knowing how deep the destruction has eaten into himself, hoping to achieve a healing juncture with his destroyed people' (p. 232). For Solo, therefore, the goal of the African writer is to fight against the oppression of Africa by Europe and America. Genuine and revolutionary creativity lies in this one central issue: ending the destruction of Africa by Europe and its American extension.

> But in the world of my people that most important first act of creation, that rearrangement without which all attempts at creation are doomed to false-ness, remains to be done. Europe hurled itself against us – not for creation, but to destroy us, to use us for creating itself. America, a growth out of Europe, now deepens that destruction. In this wreckage there is no creative art outside the destruction of the destroyers. In my people's world, revolution would be the only art, revolutionaries the only creation. All else is part of Africa's destruction. (p. 231).

In a real sense Armah makes a declaration of intent in Solo's words which appear in *Why Are We so Blest?*, and he puts it into practice in *Two Thousand Seasons*. In the latter novel, the curse of neo-colonialism in Africa is seen in its historical perspective. This historical novel criticizes foreign interference in Africa from the time of the penetration of Arab influence through the periods of slavery and colonialism to the post-independence era, when neo-colonial leaders like Kamuzu went into alliances and partnerships with 'the white destroyers' and betrayed their own people (pp. 172–3). The book not only attacks the political and economic control of Africa by Europe, but goes further to launch a bitter campaign against mental and spiritual colonization, hence the vehemence against Christianity and Islam and the assertion of the 'black is beautiful' theme. In a sense, *Two Thousand Seasons* is a fictional equivalent of Walter Rodney's *How Europe Underdeveloped Africa*, which has done more than any other document to counter the assumption that Africa benefited from Europe and would have been worse off without the latter's intervention. Of course, Rodney's book does not have the strong racial overtones of Armah's novel, and unlike Fanon who is on the side not only of Africans but also of the Arabs and the Third World in general, Armah's concept of Africa is definable strictly in terms of Black Africa since the Arabs are 'White' and are counted among the destroyers.

In *Two Thousand Seasons* we see a community of Black people struggling together against a common enemy. The unity of the Black people is asserted in very clear terms: 'That we the black people are one people we know. Destroyers will travel long distances in their minds and out to deny you this truth' (p. 3). Unity is a force which can help the African people to repulse the enemy and re-establish their control over their own destiny. In *The Healers*, which is based on the history of the Akan people of Ghana, emphasis is placed on a return to the past when the people of Ghana and of Africa are said to have been united. The past will show the people of Africa that they were not divided before; that division was a later development which can be avoided in the future. As Damfo the healer puts it, the past can inform us that 'there is nothing eternal about our present divisions. We were one in the past. We may come together again in the future' (p. 215).

From this we can conclude that Pan-Africanism and anti-neo-colonialism appear to be much stronger in Armah than socialist influences, although the latter form part of his projected social vision.

David Maillu and the Plight of the Proletariat

David Maillu is a writer who deserves greater attention from serious critics than he currently enjoys. His lighthearted style and his 'vulgar' language probably account for the critic's neglect of his writing, nevertheless his social vision is much more profound than readers may realize, for he addresses himself to some of the most serious problems facing independent Africa today. This chapter is

restricted to a brief analysis of the issues raised in *After 4.30*[10] and *My Dear
Bottle*.[11] *After 4.30* can be summarized as a book on Women's Liberation. The
protagonist of the novel, the typist, is a highly conscientized proletarian woman
who is bitterly critical of male ideology on the question of the place of women in
society. Among other things, she is no longer willing to accept the application of
the term 'prostitute' to women alone, for to her it is logical to argue that:

> If women were the prostitutes
> I'd like someone to tell me
> with whom they prostitute
> with women?
> So you see, men prostitutes
> don't consider themselves prostitutes. (p. 9)

To men, women are mere objects to be acted upon; things who owe a debt and
allegiance to men by virtue of their sex. A woman, says Lili's boss, a typical
male chauvinist, is 'a cob of maize for anyone with teeth' (p. 37). Or to put it in
more elaborate and blunt terms:

> By virtue of being a woman
> you're in a natural debt of some kind
> to pay tribute to me
> because I'm a man;
> in simpler phraseology, Lili,
> you still carry my share with you
> don't forget. (p. 38)

In this male-dominated society, women find themselves oppressed and
exploited at work, at home, everywhere. Male executives make use of their
positions as bosses to demand sex from their typists. Unless she submits to her
boss's sexual desires, a typist has no hope for promotion. And junior men, subjected to such treatment by the same women, lord it over their wives at home. In
a male-dominated bourgeois society, wives are at the beck and call of their
husbands. Those women who marry wealthy men pay for the luxury of their
homes with misery and tears. As the typist says to Mwelu, her sister:

> When you're the wife of a big man
> he expects you to take him
> like a god
> whenever you annoy him
> he threatens throwing you out
> and getting a fresh one
> to replace you (p. 67)

It is not only bosses and husbands who exploit women, but landlords as well.

These powerful exploiters not only demand sex from their women tenants, but the full rent as well so that the tenant does not have bargaining power, in spite of making use of 'THIS!' (p. 73) But the typist's concern goes beyond the cause of oppressed women. She is also aware of the contradictions of class society (pp. 110–13) and is sharply critical of neo-colonialism, corruption and hypocrisy. She is not anti-clerical, neither is she atheistic in inclination, but she delivers a telling and convincing indictment of Christian religion which, to her, is characterized by pomp and external show (pp. 113–24). Christmas has become no more than a western social convention to people, and the external symbols that go with the convention – wedding cakes, rings, garments and the like – are in any case too expensive for the poor (pp. 123–4).

In *My Dear Bottle* the protagonist is not a militant feminist, but a male drunkard. The drunkard is a member of the working class and is a failure in life. His world is a world of wishful thinking, but try as he may, he cannot emulate his boss who is himself a member of the wealthy bourgeoisie and enjoys all the advantages that accrue to those who belong to that class, including the use of big cars like the Mercedes Benz. In many ways, the drunkard is the male equivalent of the typist in *After 4.30*. Like the typist, he is a spokesman for the less privileged section of the population, and he is similarly far from idealized. He makes it clear that if he were in power he would indulge in corrupt practices (pp. 37–8). Nevertheless, what he says about what he would get up to were he a minister is meant to be a reflection of the corruption of those in the upper echelons of society. Thus Maillu takes a drunkard, who himself has faults, and criticizes the injustices of society through him.

But Maillu's probing goes even deeper than that. He is also concerned with the whole question of the causes of the drunkard's behaviour. What is it that causes this uncontrolled drinking, in other words? The protagonist himself provides the answer:

> Man, I drink
> to drink up my sorrows
> and my frustrations.
> My friend, the bottle tells me
> the right kind of lies
> that I'm a rich man.
> I drink to brighten my eyes.
> Beer is good for brushing clean
> your interior corners of distress.
> It's good
> because it gives you the hope
> that you'll still survive.
> Without hope, man
> you're dead (pp. 59–60).

This is the outcry of a man in despair. Underneath the writer's apparent lightheartedness there is a genuinely serious concern with the material conditions of life, with the ultimate source of such disreputable behaviour as the drunkard's, and that is the unequal distribution of wealth, the absence of care for certain sections of the population. The protagonist is not as highly conscientized as the typist in *After 4.30*, but Maillu clearly wants his readers to sympathize with drunkards in the same way as he wants them to sympathize with prostitutes.

The drunkard's friend has clear ideas about equality and human exploitation (p. 82). The friend is a very progressive thinker whose ideas transcend the pettiness of narrow nationalism, tradition and racism in favour of the common humanity of all mankind (pp. 118–19). Implicit in his argument is an acceptance of the ideals of revolutionary internationalism and a rejection of bourgeois nationalism and reactionary chauvinism.[12] Maillu chooses a more enlightened character to voice such progressive ideas, because the drunkard does not have the level of consciousness necessary to articulate them in this way. It is through this same friend that the writer is able to deliver one of the sharpest and most direct criticisms of capitalist Kenya. Commenting on the decision of the authorities to destroy Mathare Valley, a shanty town, the drunkard finds himself quoting his friend in the following words:

> My friend commented something
> about Mathare Valley shanties.
> He said that he failed to understand
> what the fuss was all about
> when Mathare Valley was only the reflection
> of how the majority of the people
> lived in the country (p. 135).

The description of the drunkard's relative who lived in the Valley 'on illegal brew of Chang'aa' once again highlights Maillu's commitment not only to the workers, but to the lumpen-proletariat as well (pp. 130–5).

In the final analysis, however, Maillu's novels cannot be described as 'socialist art'. His final word on socialism is pronounced by the drunkard's learned friend who is critical of both capitalism and socialism. The major criticism against communism, or what he calls 'another form of capitalism where a chosen élite must control the entire population', is that its rulers exercise their power through fear (p. 137). Though he is a radical writer who sides with the workers and the less privileged sections of society, his position is no more than that of a social critic; he does not examine the possibility of collective bargaining for the workers, or define the problem in terms of the class struggle. However, the point must be made that Maillu's writings draw their strength from proletarian culture and should find a place among the works of those who are committed to the cause of the less privileged classes of bourgeois society. He may with some justification be condemned as a 'pornographic jester', but his style should not obscure the fact that he raises questions capable of pricking the consciences of those in positions of power and authority.

Ngugi and the Awakening of the Masses

From an ideological standpoint Ngugi's transformation during the course of his writing career has been gradual but decisive. Between 1964, when his first novel was published, and 1977 when *Petals of Blood* saw the light of day, Ngugi's ideological perspective has developed from nationalist politics to revolutionary politics, from critical realism to socialist art. A brief look at his four novels first written in English will reveal this ideological transformation.

In *Weep Not, Child*,[13] his first novel, Ngugi is already aware of the class differences between the rising petty-bourgeoisie, represented by Jacobo's family, and the poor unpropertied peasants, represented by Ngotho's family. But although it shows that the author is a militant writer, *Weep Not, Child* is not a socialist novel. The book very successfully dramatizes the events of Mau Mau, but the wider implications and results of the war are forgotten in the concentration on the dark days and tragedy of certain individual families. The global significance of the ideological conflict that gives rise to Mau Mau is lost and the protagonist manifests clear signs of ideological bankruptcy, for Njoroge believes in the illusion that education is the answer to the social evils of his society, and when the forces of oppression and reaction deprive him of the opportunity to be highly educated, he is so completely disillusioned that he entertains the romantic idea of running away from Kenya with the girl he loves, and actually ends up in despair, attempting to commit suicide. A very grim ending indeed. Lenin might say that Ngugi misunderstood the Mau Mau movement by introducing a strong element of despair into his novel, for 'despair is typical of those who do not understand the causes of evil, see no way out, and are incapable of struggle'.[14]

The River Between[15] is, like many other African novels of the period, a critique of colonialism and western Christianity. It works at the level of nationalist politics: Black versus White, the colonized versus the colonialist, African tradition versus western civilization. The main character, Waiyaki, follows the conventional pattern of a leading figure in a bourgeois novel. He is a hero in the true sense of the word, towering above the ordinary man and woman in the village. He is someone special, a leading figure like Achebe's heroes – Okonkwo, Obi, Ezeulu. The original title of *The River Between* was *The Black Messiah*. A messiah is not an ordinary person, and so Waiyaki, who was supposed to bear that title, was not meant to be an ordinary person.

In *A Grain of Wheat*,[16] Ngugi shows his socialist inclinations by focusing his attention on the common people and their predicament. The novel depicts the events leading to the coming of Uhuru, but the focus is not on the major events that are recorded in history books. Kenyatta is mentioned, but only as part of the history of the people of Kenya – Ngugi does not project the interests and views of outstanding figures like Kenyatta and other people in the upper echelons of society. The book talks about independence celebrations, but we are not shown the celebrations which took place in Nairobi, the capital city of Kenya. Rather, we are taken to an insignificant place out in the country –

Thabai. Similarly, the characters we deal with are small village people and members of the peasant class – Gikonyo, Gitogo, Mumbi, Karanja and, of course, their British overlords.

We witness here colonial Kenya giving way to the independent Republic of Kenya which is the result of the sacrifices of the people of Kenya who suffered and died for freedom's sake. As the Bible quotation prefixed to the beginning of Chapter 14 suggests, there was in Kenya 'a new heaven and a new earth; for the first heaven and the first earth were passed away'. But the crucial question is whether Uhuru has brought forth much fruit as a result of the people who died. In other words, has independence brought about a change of system for the better?

This is the point at which Ngugi projects the point of view, not of the new rulers, but of the peasants. The evidence in the book suggests that the peasants are disappointed by the kind of Uhuru they get. They suffered in order to achieve freedom for all, but after Uhuru ministers of state are no longer interested in those who put them in power. The MP for Thabai does not even go home to celebrate with the people in his rural constituency. Not only that, Gikonyo and his colleagues work very hard to raise money in order to buy a farm from a certain Mr Burton; but when they have raised the money what do they find? Their own MP has bought the farm. They are utterly disappointed. It is the bureaucratic bourgeoisie who reap the fruits of independence, not the people. Gikonyo goes further and asks: would Uhuru bring land into African hands? And would that make a difference to the small man in the village? Ngugi's peasants here ask the same questions which the writer has put more directly in the essay *The Writer in a Changing Society*: 'What have these peasants gained from Uhuru? Has our ruling élite tried to change the colonial social and economic structure? Are the peasants and workers in control of the land they worked for?'[17] The answer to all these questions is 'no'. For as Ngugi puts it elsewhere, 'the masses are realizing that Blackness is not all'.[18]

In *A Grain of Wheat*, therefore, Ngugi has managed to put the question, although he does not provide any solution in clear-cut terms. But if the masses have realized that blackness is not all, that for Ngugi is 'a glimmer of hope'.[19] The hope is expressed obscurely in terms of a sophisticated para-linguistic affective device, which appears in the last section of Chapter 14. Dathorne has argued that the stool which Gikonyo decides to carve and present as a wedding gift to Mumbi is a symbol of future life and productivity.[20] At one point Gikonyo contemplates carving 'a field needing clearance and cultivation' or 'a bean flower'. These are symbols of fertility. In the end he decides to carve a woman 'big-big with child'; in other words, a pregnant woman. This can be interpreted as a symbol of fruitful Kenya – Kenya is portrayed as a pregnant mother, a mother who will give birth to life. In other words, Kenya will bear fruit in the end, just as the relations between Gikonyo and Mumbi return to normal in the end. This is Ngugi's faith in the soil which he sees as the source of hope for unity in his motherland: 'Perhaps the soil, which in the traditional view was always seen as a source of creative life and fertility, will unite them. In this lies the hope of Kenya.'[21] But even here the solution proposed is vague for it is not precisely clear as to how the soil will solve Kenya's problems.

For a more coherently formulated view of the future of Kenya, we should turn to *Petals of Blood*,[22] where Ngugi's social vision is articulated in clearly defined Marxist terms. *A Grain of Wheat* is a transitional novel marking Ngugi's development from nationalist politics and critical realism to revolutionary politics and socialist art. By the time he wrote *Petals of Blood*, he was firmly set on the socialist revolution and the antagonistic forces in his society were crystal clear to him. He completed the novel after a visit to the Soviet Union where he presumably received inspiration from the Soviet Union of Writers. *Petals of Blood* is a milestone in the development of socialist art in Africa and is the subject of a full chapter in this book.

Notes

1 *The Historical Novel*, p. 204.
2 *Violence* and *Firebrands* are both publications of Longman Drumbeat.
3 *Two Thousand Seasons*, London, Heinemann African Writers Series 218, 1979.
4 *Myth, Literature and the African World*, pp. 106–108.
5 Ibid., pp. 111–12.
6 *The Healers*, Nairobi, East African Publishing House, 1978, pp. 342–3.
7 *Why Are We So Blest?* London, Heinemann African Writers Series 155, 1974, p. 114.
8 *Myth, Literature and the African World*, p. 112.
9 *The Wretched of the Earth*, p. 134.
10 *After 4.30*. Nairobi, Comb Books, 1974.
11 *My Dear Bottle*, Nairobi, Comb Books, 1973.
12 See *The Fundamentals of Marxist-Leninist Philosophy*, Progress Publishers, pp. 398–9.
13 *Weep Not, Child*, London, Heinemann African Writers Series 7, 1964.
14 See 'L. N. Tolstoy and the Modern Labour Movement', in V. I. Lenin, *On Literature and Art*, p. 51.
15 *The River Between*, London, Heinemann African Writers Series 17, 1965.
16 *A Grain of Wheat*, London, Heinemann African Writers Series 36, 1967.
17 See *Homecoming*, p. 49.
18 Ibid., p. 56.
19 Ibid., p. 56.
20 See *African Literature in the Twentieth Century*.
21 *Homecoming*, p. 25.
22 *Petals of Blood*, London, Heinemann African Writers Series 188, 1977.

7   The Development of Proletarian Consciousness: Ousmane's God's Bits of Wood

▼▼▼▼▼▼▼▼▼▼▼▼▼▼▼▼▼▼▼▼▼▼▼▼▼▼▼▼▼▼▼▼

Consciousness and Class Struggle

On a superficial level, *God's Bits of Wood*[1] is a novel about the power of collective bargaining. Schneider has summarized the functions of a trade union in the following words:

> As we have seen, the first, and in many ways primary, function of the trade union is to create and wield power which, within the legal processes of the country, can be used to bring management to terms. Its second major function is to bargain collectively with management about these terms.[2]

And Hyman's definition of a strike is 'a temporary stoppage of work by a group of employees in order to express a grievance or enforce a demand'.[3]

On the face of it, Ousmane's story, which is based on the 1947–8 strike of the railway workers on the Dakar-Niger line in the then French West Africa, would seem to be very much in line with the two functions outlined above and with Hyman's definition of a strike. There is a conflict between the management of the Dakar-Niger line and the railway workers' union, and the union is not officially recognized by the management. Some of the major demands of the strikers are clearly articulated on the banners of the women of Thiès as they stage their triumphant march into Dakar, with slogans like: *We demand family allowances   For equal work – equal pay   Old age pensions, and Proper housing,* etc. (p. 212). When the management refuses to grant these and other demands, the railway workers resort to a strike.

But Sembène Ousmane's novel goes beyond the scope of an ordinary stoppage. The conflict is couched in Marxist terms and is presented as a class struggle between those who control the means of production and the exploited working class. True, there is no indication that the strike will develop into a political agitation for full national independence and the liquidation of colonialism, nor is there any suggestion that the workers are poised for a violent overthrow of exploitative capitalism. On the contrary, the strikers call off their strike as soon as their demands are met. However, the strike takes on the characteristics of a class struggle. It is an instance of the continual agitation of the oppressed working class against the ruling class. It was Marx who said:

> Where the working class is not yet far enough advanced in its organisation to undertake a decisive campaign against the collective power, that is, the political power, of the ruling classes, it must at any rate be trained for this by continual agitation against the policy of the ruling classes and adopting an attitude hostile to it.[4]

But the railway men's strike becomes something much greater than an example of continual agitation. If they were not aware of their fundamental interests before the strike, the strikers, their women, children and fellow workers emerge from it with a high degree of political consciousness and have gone through experiences characteristic of liberation struggles. In the following pages I will endeavour to show how Ousmane achieves this.

First, the chief participants in the conflict display some of the characteristics of their respective classes. Dejean and other members of the management, representatives of the bourgeoisie, claim that they represent a nation, as if France, the nation in question, is inhabited by one class of people with a common goal and common interests. Dejean accordingly accuses Lahbib of insulting 'a great nation and a great people'. But Lahbib is an ideologized member of the working class and is swift in refuting the false pretences with 'You do not represent a nation or a people here, but simply a class. We represent another class, whose interests are not the same as yours' (p. 182).

An important function of the labour movement from a Marxist point of view is its commitment to revolutionary internationalism. As Fischer puts it, 'Labour movements must also intervene in the foreign policies of their respective countries'.[5] The strikers and their families are able to carry on with their struggle largely as a result of the financial help they receive from comrades in other countries, including France itself (pp. 184, 218). This is a complete negation of the claims of Dejean and his associates that they represent the nation of France. What they do represent, in terms of the novel, is the ruling class which controls the means of production and the French colonies.

A very important feature of the theme of class struggle in the book is the growing consciousness of the oppressed classes. This increasing understanding of their state of existence is a skilful expression of the Marxist idea of consciousness as articulated in *A Preface to a Contribution to the Critique of Political Economy*, where Marx says:

> It is not the consciousness of men that determines their existence, but, on the contrary, it is their social existence that determines their consciousness. At a certain stage of their development the material productive forces of society come into contradiction with the existing productive relationships . . . . From forms of development of the productive forces these relationships are transformed into their fetters. Then an epoch of social revolution opens.[6]

Therefore the social conditions of the toiling and exploited worker in *God's Bits of Wood* give rise to social agitation expressed in the form of a strike, and the experience of striking raises the level of political awareness not only in the conscientized young workers but also in the minds of their women folk and the older generation of men. The strike is organized by the younger workers, but gradually their agitation begins to open the minds of the older men so that old Bakary becomes acutely aware of the injustice of a system which gives pensions to Whites and refuses them to Blacks: 'Why should we not have this pension, too? This is what the young ones are asking' (p. 18).

Of much greater significance is the rising consciousness in the women of their own state of oppression in their feudalistic society and the need for them to participate in matters that affect them, their husbands and their children. Thus Houdia M'baye's child who is born during the strike is called Strike – a mark of the women's awakening and of their identifying with their husbands' course of action. But it is not only the women who become conscious of their new role; their men also begin to understand that 'if the times were bringing forth a new breed of men, they were also bringing forth a new breed of women' (p. 34).

The rising consciousness of the women is first determined by the prevailing material conditions – the need for food and drink when all the supplies are cut and men can no longer bring bread to their families. The women's new role resulting from the circumstances is neatly summed up by Mame Sofi: 'You'll see – the men will consult us before they go out on another strike. Before this, they thought they owned the earth just because they feed us, but now it is the women who are feeding them' (p. 47). After this, women get more and more involved in the affairs of their society. They participate in a meeting for the first time, to the utter shock and amazement of their men. They have successful confrontations with the police and soldiers and, most important of all, the women of Thiès take the initiative to launch a heroic march to Dakar. The success of the strike is due, in large measure, to the action of these heroic women, for it is 'the marchers' who are finally responsible for the coming together of all groups of workers, who declare a general strike which brings the company in the end to its knees (pp. 211, 219).

Revolutionary struggles and class struggles are marked by violence, and violence is a significant feature of the novel under discussion. The more the strike gathers momentum the more ruthless the instruments of oppression become. Hence not only are the strikers and their families deprived of the basic necessities of life – food and water – but many of them die in the struggle – Niakoro, Doudou, Samba, Houdia M'baye, Penda and others. There is so much death that even the man of metal, Bakayoko, is overcome by depression and pessimism (p. 211).

At the same time, the ruling class, in an attempt to dissuade the population from supporting the agitators, will always label their actions 'communist inspired'. In other words, the workers and peasants are depicted as incapable of thinking for themselves and only acting on the instigation of 'foreign' communists who are anti-Christian or anti-Islamic. To strengthen its own position, the ruling class will enlist on its side respectable individuals, religious and lay, who have been absorbed into the privileged bourgeois class and are displayed as shining examples of virtue, civilization and material success. This is the position of El Hadji Mabigué, the Imam and the Black mayor-deputy of Dakar (p. 219). On the question of communists the Imam, a representative of the Moslem religion, has this to say:

It is time you understood that your husbands are just the instruments of a band of infidels who are using them for their own purposes. It is the Communists who are really directing this strike, and if you knew and understood the things that happen in their country you would pray to God that he might forgive them. They speak to you of famine, but in their own country there is constant famine. Their laws are the laws of heretics who permit a brother to sleep with his sister – tell your husbands that (p. 124).

Here we see the alliance between capitalism and the church which is a familiar feature of bourgeois society.

Ousmane does not, however, regard all religious people as reactionary and treacherous. The conventional religious outlook of the Imam is in sharp contrast to that of the deeply religious old man, Fa Keita. Fa Keita, a symbol of traditional wisdom and Islamic virtue, is evidently a holy man who cannot forget his prayers and his God, be he in the quiet of his home or the darkness of a filthy prison. But the old man participates in the strike, playing an advisory role, and he gets his fair share of suffering, for he loses his wife, Niakoro, and suffers the indignity of savage imprisonment.

Two important observations may be made about the theme of growing consciousness in *God's Bits of Wood*. First, Sembène Ousmane has prophetically expressed in the art form of the novel what has since actually taken place in some liberation struggles in Africa. In Zimbabwe, women in the now ruling ZANU-PF party became more and more outspoken about the oppression of women, not only in colonial and capitalist Rhodesia, but also in traditional Shona society, which was feudalistic and characterized by the subordination of woman to man. During the liberation struggle, women guerrillas fought alongside their male comrades, and eventually even non-combatants became so vocal about the necessity to agitate for the liberation of women simultaneously with the armed struggle that the party began to realize the importance of giving high positions to women – hence the rise of such figures as Teurai Ropa Nhongo, the Minister of Community Development and Women's Affairs, Victoria Chitepo, the Minister of Tourism and Natural Resources and Naomi Nhiwatiwa, the Deputy Minister of Information, Posts and Telecommunications.

Secondly, the novel shows clearly that the workers and their women are not simply automatons acting under the spell of history. Theirs is 'conscious activity of conscious men'.[7] The workers need the organizational skill of Lahbib and Bakayoko. To be successful they need the energy and intellectual acumen of Bakayoko. For the march of the women to succeed, the leadership qualities and untiring dedication of Penda are required. The exploited masses of French West Africa have indeed become conscious of their existence as a result of the relations of production, but they are not driven blindly to their success by the inexorable march of history. Individuals react to the situation differently according to their own being, talent and level of political consciousness. Thus, while the majority of workers join in the strike, Sounkare, the watchman, chooses the opposite course; and privileged individuals like El Hadji Mabigué are used by the company and the state apparatus to frustrate the efforts of the strikers. These men and women are therefore not driven like robots by history. They also act upon and create history. As Fischer so neatly puts it:

> Revolutionary practice changes circumstances and changes man himself. It sees man not only as the object of history but also as its subject: he is an object capable, by subjective activity, of becoming a subject and of changing existing circumstances.[8]

Sembène Ousmane seems to understand the dialectics of revolutionary practice very well and hence, in the note at the beginning of the book, he implicitly tells us that the men and women who took part in the strike of 1947–8 made history, for 'their example was not in vain. Since then, Africa has made progress'.

Language and Readability

In discussing the language component of the linguistic format of the novel, the present critic is at a disadvantage, for not only is the edition under discussion a translation, but he cannot read French, and therefore misses the rhythms and nuances of the original language articulated by Sembène Ousmane. The other component of the linguistic format – the level of para-linguistic affective devices – is much more accessible in translation. And so we venture to comment on the style of *God's Bits of Wood*, aware all the time that something is always lost in translation and what we read partly reflects the linguistic talents of the translator.

On the face of it, the novel does not have very striking linguistic features. It is rather like Ngugi's *A Grain of Wheat*, whose linguistic format does not strike the reader in the same way as, say, Armah's *Two Thousand Seasons*. But this in itself is no problem to the stylistic critic, for stylistic criticism is concerned with significant features, features which add to the aesthetic quality of the novel, or which reveal the author's artistic vision. With regard to the author's artistic concerns, it is quite clear that Sembène Ousmane is acutely aware of the problem of writing in French when depicting the lives and experiences of people who are themselves not French-speaking or who alternate from one language to another, depending on the situation. This is shown by the fact that the author frequently takes it upon himself to comment on the language used by a character in the course of a dialogue. But the revelation of character through the use of language is evidently not one of the major preoccupations of the author, and so a socio-linguistic study of the relationship between language and character would be a futile exercise. However, there are several other stylistic features which are worthy of note.

Ousmane's style is in the main *concrete*, i.e. he tends to convey his message through the depiction of episode, character and dialogue rather than through the discussion of abstract ideas. Relying on concrete images, Ousmane is capable of using very forceful language, particularly in passages where he records a violent clash. Here is an example:

That was when the soldiers charged.

The battle was joined in an instant, and with every available weapon: the butt-ends of muskets, the tips of bayonets, the soles of heavy boots, and tear-gas bombs. Cries of rage, of pain, and of fear mingled in single clamour, rising to the morning sky. The crowd fell back, breaking into terrified segments, then regrouped, wavered, and fell back again. Dieynaba had rallied the women of the market place, and like a band of Amazons they came to the rescue, armed with clubs, with iron bars and bottles. . . . In the market place itself, not a single stall remained standing; the conflict was everywhere at once (p. 22).

There is power and poetry in these words, but Ousmane can rise to even greater poetic heights, particularly in the closing paragraphs of some of his chapters where he goes beyond the level of a powerful description in concrete images to a conceptual style. Here is such a passage:

Ad'jibid'ji disappeared down the corridor, and the old people were left alone in their thoughts and fears. The night no longer brought them rest. At the moment the eyes of the body closed, the eyes of the mind were opened. On the threshold of every dwelling place, people listened to the distant rhythm of the dance. In the darkness that enclosed the city the deep-toned drumming seemed now to come from everywhere at once, twisting and turning through the heads of those to whom sleep would not come (p. 12).

And here is another:

Only once each week did the 'smoke of the savanna' rise above the brush, from the trains run by the Europeans, on those days the strikers would stop whatever they were doing and turn their heads to listen, like hunted animals startled by an unwanted sound. For a moment, the passage of the locomotive would calm the torment in their hearts, because their fellowship with the machine was deep and strong; stronger than the barriers which separated them from their employers, stronger even than the obstacle which until now had been insurmountable – the colour of their skin.

Then the smoke would disappear, and there would be only silence again, or
the sighing of the wind (pp. 76–7)

In these passages Ousmane's style rises to the level of the conceptual, to a point
where he is no longer simply descriptive, but where he is striving to penetrate
into the depths of the human psyche, to probe the thinking processes of the
masses of French West Africa who are compelled by the circumstances to contemplate on their present predicament, to reflect on their social conditions. This
is part and parcel of his preoccupation with the problem of consciousness, with
the new social psychology which the new productive forces, symbolized by the
machine, have generated in a period of social upheaval. Thus the workers are
not only acted upon by the machine, in the sense that the machine has changed
their social being; they also contemplate it, becoming subjects to the object of
the machine – an intimation of the impending ascendancy of the workers to
economic power.

Here, finally, is a passage where, in one sentence, Ousmane manages to
combine concrete symbols: tarbooshes, the river and the sea, with a philosophical conception of the march of the women of Thiès who have broken
through a barricade of soldiers: 'But how could a handful of men in red tarbooshes prevent this great river from rolling on to the sea?' (p. 202).

In this one sentence alone, Ousmane succeeds in portraying the proletariat as
a force which the state apparatus of colonial bourgeois society cannot control.
As in Armah's *Two Thousand Seasons*, the river is a symbol of the particular and
the sea of the universal. The Senegal River is characterized by particularity – it
belongs to the specific region of West Africa – but the Atlantic Ocean into which
it flows is universal: it belongs to no land and no continent. The marching
women are here identified with the river, for their march is from the hinterland
to the edge of the sea, just as the flow of the Senegal is from the hinterland to the
edge of the sea. The sea here assumes a special significance: 'In the last miles
before they reached their goal they passed a point from which they could see the
island of Gorée, a tiny black dot in the great expanse of the ocean' (p. 201). But if
the river and the sea are significant, what else can they stand for in this context
except for the idea that the struggle of the masses of French West Africa is linked
with the aims and purposes of universal insurgence?

In terms of readability, Ousmane's narrative is good but it does not have the
compelling power of, say, Soyinka's *Season of Anomy*. This is largely the result
of the narrative structure and the author's handling of characterization. The
events are not told through the consciousness of one or several characters with
whom the reader can identify. Instead, we have a multiplicity of characters
underlining the collective nature of the struggle. The character who dominates
the strike, Bakayoko, is a distant, Olympian figure who the reader 'hears about'
and does not actually encounter until the narrative is moving to its climax. The
reader can to some extent identify with such characters as Ka Feita, Penda and
Bakayoko himself, but the suspense that one experiences in some novels as a
result of anxiety to know the fate of a character is not a strong feature of this

particular novel. The reader identifies not with an individual, but with the exploited class striving for justice. And so what spurs the reader on are the dynamics of the story itself, the desire to see the resolution to the conflict.

Para-linguistic Affective Devices

Ousmane uses a number of very significant para-linguistic affective devices. The most obvious one is the *Legend of Goumba*, which is derived from African folklore. Maimouna sings the following verses:

'I have come to take a wife,' the stranger said.
'My bridegroom must be stronger than I, there are my father's
fields,
And there are the abandoned scythes,' replied Goumba N'Diaye.
And the stranger took up a scythe.
Two days each week, and still they came not to the end,
But the man could not vanquish the girl (p. 21)

For two moons they cleared the land,
And neither the stranger nor Goumba N'Diaye would confess to
being vanquished
Beat on all the drums!
'Stranger,' demanded Goumba N'Diaye, 'From what country do
you come?'
And the stranger replied, 'I am from every country.
I am a man like every man'
'It is not true', said Goumba N'Diaye
'For many seasons, men have fled from me.
Men are not alike' (p. 22)

The first verse expresses a very common theme in African folklore: to acquire a treasure you must work and toil for it, to possess a beautiful bride you must vanquish Goumba N'Diaye in order to win her, but alas 'the man could not vanquish the girl'.

In the context of the novel the legend assumes a new significance. The struggle between the girl and the stranger is symbolic of the titanic struggle between the railway company and the strikers, between the bourgeoisie and the proletariat, between capitalism and socialism. The company, the bourgeoisie and capitalism are symbolized by the stubborn girl, Goumba N'Diaye, and the railway workers, the proletariat and socialism by the stranger. This interpretation becomes clear if one looks closely at the second verse where the stranger says he is 'a man like every man'. These are the workers of the world whom Marx called upon to unite. This is the revolutionary class which is destined to demolish the fabric of capitalism.

By enriching his style with a song from a traditional legend, Ousmane pays tribute to his ancestors. But there is more to it than a backward look to the wisdom of the forefathers. By juxtaposing the two songs, one from oral traditions and a modern one created at a time of social crisis, Ousmane is highlighting one of the major principles operating in the novel – a fusion of the positive elements of traditional life and the new revolutionary culture arising from the new social awareness. It may be noted that the revolutionary song born on 10 October is improvized by women who are under the leadership of Penda (p. 172) and that the song of the *Legend of Goumba* is sung by Maimouna, the blind woman. It may also be noted that both songs are carried by the marchers from Thiès to Dakar (pp. 218–19). This is no mere coincidence. The marriage of the two songs symbolizes a synthesis of the old and the new. The *Legend of Goumba* is a prophetic voice buried deep in the traditions of the ancestors, a voice which finds fulfilment in the new voice of the emerging revolutionary woman born on 10 October 1947. The prophetic nature of the song is shown by the fact that it is sung by a blind woman who can see the truth without seeing the world. But Maimouna is not simply a blind commentator, a living embodiment of the ways of the fathers uprooted by colonialism, but also a Tiresias who unites the past, the present and the future.[9] On one level Maimouna is Ousmane's equivalent of Eliot's Tiresias, who 'though blind' can see.[10] And we can say of Maimouna what Eliot says of his Tiresias that what she sees 'in fact, is the substance' of the novel.[11]

The synthesis of the two elements, the traditional and the revolutionary, is symbolized in physical terms by Penda and the blind woman sharing the same roof (pp. 137–8). It is after this that Penda is involved in the strike, eventually getting so committed that she becomes the standard bearer, leading a formidable army of revolutionary women on their way to the citadel of the enemy, Dakar. It is noteworthy that the blind woman who one would expect to be incapacitated in the struggle or to be hindered by her physical handicaps from undertaking the strenuous journey, marches with the rest of the women right into Dakar and even surviving those, like Penda, who are shot dead on their arrival in the city. So the blind woman is not just a blind woman, she is not even just a Tiresias who sees and comments. She is an ancestral spirit following the new race of women, shielding them and giving them spiritual support and the nourishment that comes from an awareness of the wisdom bequeathed to them by the fathers of old.

It is noteworthy that at the beginning of the novel the blind woman has twins, one of whom dies in the clash between the soldiers and the masses of Thiès. In the ensuing pandemonium the other twin is also threatened with death, but the old woman clutches her to her breast 'her arched back forming a shield' (p. 23). The twins are clearly a symbol of the new breed of men and women who are engaged in a struggle with the forces of oppression. The one who dies foreshadows those who are going to fall, the heroes of the struggle, while the surviving child represents the living who emerge victorious at the end of the day under the protective shield of the ancestors.

Another important symbol in the novel is 'the machine'. If the song of the marchers and the *Legend of Goumba* symbolize the ideology of the future, 'the machine' (i.e. the train) is a symbol of the technology of the future, a technology which the masses of Africa should accept and master if their countries are to develop into modern states. There is a frequent reference in the book to 'the machine' which is associated with the strikers. The significance of the train is symbolized by the fact that as soon as the news of the successful end of the strike reaches his ears, Bakayoko orders Tiemoko to drive a train from Bamako to Thiès, and indeed the arrival of Tiemoko in Thiès heralds the end of the strike and the beginning of life (pp. 241–2). The *Legend of Goumba*, the women's revolutionary song and 'the machine' stand for a synthesis of the old and the new. This is borne out by the following passage in which Ousmane depicts the striking men contemplating 'the machine' which they know to be 'the source of their common welfare':

> Something was being born inside them, as if the past and the future were coupling to breed a new kind of man, and it seemed to them that the wind was whispering a phrase they had often heard from Bakayoko: 'The kind of man we were is dead, and our only hope for a new life lies in the machine, which knows neither a language nor a race' (p. 76).

The Narrative Structure

Ousmane's concern with art shows itself in the design of the novel. The map attached to the beginning of the book is of great help to the reader. It helps him to comprehend more clearly the author's handling of the narrative structure, which takes the form of a series of events in different places along the whole Dakar-Niger line. The chapters are not numbered. Instead, there is simply a heading and a sub-heading, the former indicating the town where the scene takes place, and the latter the name of the main character in the particular scene. Thus we move from Bamako, to Thiès, to Dakar and back to Bamako, etc. The focus is always on one of these towns and the drama finally ends in Thiès.

This narrative structure enables Ousmane to present a series of sub-plots which are linked by the common features of the strike, the union and Bakayoko. As the railway line links the towns in physical terms, so the union and its soul Bakayoko, link the events which take place in these different places and are brought together by the march of the women of Thiès, whose triumphant entry into Dakar brings together all the antagonistic forces in the conflict. The march of the women ends with a neat dramatization of the ideological conflict. There are two clear camps: on the one hand are the company officials, government officials and all the collaborators; and on the other is the exploited class – the railwaymen, fishermen, dock workers, workers from all the big factories in the city and, of course, the marchers (p. 211).

On another level, the structure of the novel resembles certain forms of traditional folklore. There are a number of stories taking place in different places, rather similar to the stories in Tutuola's *The Palm-Wine Drinkard*. The novel is therefore not about one or two main characters, which is the usual technique. Ousmane's book is about a whole community of workers. This approach not only agrees with the idea of African communalism, but reflects socialist ideology, which focuses on people rather than individuals. In this way Ousmane departs radically from the bourgeois novel with its emphasis on the hero. But a people must have leaders, a struggle must have its ideologists – hence the importance of Bakayoko and the other leaders.

Characterization

In seeking to encompass a wide spectrum of the people involved in the strike without restricting himself to the experiences of a few selected individuals, Ousmane runs the risk of presenting flat characters standing for types, rather than fully developed characters. This is probably true of the majority of the participants in the drama, like Lahbib, Ramatoulaye, Sounkare and Doudou. But some of the major characters do develop. Take, for instance, Beaugosse, who is initially presented as a revolutionary intellectual trusted by the workers. Beaugosse's fear of and hatred for Bakayoko grows into a hatred for the strike, and our revolutionary intellectual ends up a renegade and a collaborator with the enemy. Penda, 'the prostitute', is gradually drawn into the struggle and eventually becomes the driving force behind the women's revolution. She becomes a revolutionary leader and dies a hero's death. Then there is Bakayoko himself, the moving spirit of the strike. Ousmane presents him as a mysterious figure whose name is on the lips of the strikers from Sudan to Senegal, from Bamako to Dakar. This is how the reader first encounters the hero – from what the other characters say – and when he finally meets him in the second half of the novel, the reader is struck by the qualities of this strange man of genius whose personality is both enchanting and bewildering. He is enchanting because he is an exceptionally talented revolutionary. Not only does he show an amazing understanding of the dynamics of social change, not only is he clear about the nature of the ideological conflict the workers have set in motion (p. 182), but he is also an orator, an intelligent speaker who disarms the management of the Dakar-Niger company as well as the governor-general and other members of the ruling class and their associates. He is bewildering because he has a heart of stone, incapable of being moved by events that touch the hearts of other men. He makes no attempt to please, show sympathy or affection to those who admire him, advise him or love him. When his uncle, Bakary, informs him of the death of his mother, his reaction is shocking to the old man. 'We must fight for the living and not give our time to thinking of the dead,' he says. The pretty girl, N'Deye Touti, is torn between her love for Bakayoko and her love for Beaugosse. She is even bribed by the highest colonial authorities so that she may choose Beaugosse, the renegade, and is given a place among the state dignitaries on the day of the great meeting, but after all the speeches she resolves her own problem independently and openly declares her love for Bakayoko. But Bakayoko deserts her and leaves her broken-hearted, though her contact with him leaves her with a sense of commitment to humanity (pp. 222–4).

In the long run, however, not even this stone-hearted man can be unaffected by the lessons of the strike. He is moved to sorrow by the number of people who lose their lives in the struggle and is particularly touched by Penda's death. And when he finally returns home, his relations with his wife, Assitan, are no longer what they were. For the first time she feels 'a warmth, a joy she had never known before' (p. 235). The relations between Bakayoko and Assitan are similar to those between Gikonyo and Mumbi at the end of *A Grain of Wheat*. Thus the strike in *God's Bits of Wood* is a lesson for all.

Conclusion

In conclusion, it is important to emphasize that Sembène Ousmane is not only concerned with socio-political issues, that he is not only projecting socialist ideology, but is also alive to the need to project his social vision in a genuinely artistic form. He is presenting both a philosophy of life and a philosophy of art. The fusion of the traditional and the modern which has been referred to, the return to the *Legend of Goumba* in a modern socialist novel is a practical application of the Marxist principle that 'the art of the various socialist countries each has socialism as its content, but each has its own national character'.[12]

On the sociological level, Ousmane successfully demonstrates that the strike has generated a new social psychology, marking a new level of socio-political awareness and a tendency towards democracy, justice and progress. The workers have positively rejected the exploitation of man by man. The women have broken the chains of their psychological and social domination by men, and their men – Bakayoko included – have come to accept this. The masses of French West Africa have also come to the realization that their language and culture are not inferior to French language and culture – hence the emphasis on Ouolof and the return to old ceremonies and customs long forgotten (p. 75). Indeed, the new awareness is an expression of the fact that 'the masses do not want to go on living in the old way, that the existing conditions have become intolerable and should be changed'.[13]

Notes

1 *God's Bits of Wood*, London, Heinemann African Writers Series 63, 1976 (first published in French as *Les Bouts de Bois de Dieu* in 1960).
2 E. V. Schneider, *Industrial Sociology*, p. 301.
3 R. Hyman, *Strikes*, p. 17.
4 E. Fischer, *Marx in His Own Words*, p. 88.

5 Ibid., p. 146.

6 E. Fromm, *Marx's Concept of Man*, pp. 217–18.

7 Fischer, ibid., p. 86.

8 Ibid., p. 92.

9 For a discussion of T. S. Eliot's *Tiresias* see Ngara's M Phil thesis, 'The Significance of Time and Motion in the Poetry of T. S. Eliot: With Special Reference to the Teaching of Eliot in Rhodesia', pp. 87 ff.

10 T. S. Eliot, *Collected Poems 1909–1962*, p. 71.

11 Ibid., p. 82.

12 S. Stuart, *Mao Tse-Tung Unrehearsed: Talks and Letters 1956–1971*, p. 84.

13 *The Fundamentals of Marxist-Leninist Philosophy*, Moscow, Progress Publishers, p. 471.

8 Towards a New Socialist Order: Ngugi's Petals of Blood

▼▼▼▼▼▼▼▼▼▼▼▼▼▼▼▼▼▼▼▼▼▼▼▼▼▼▼

Introduction to Theme

From the point of view of both theme and time perspective, *Petals of Blood*[1] begins where *A Grain of Wheat*[2] stops. At the time of his arrest Munira, one of the four main characters, has been in Ilmorog for twelve years and one policeman remarks that Munira must have arrived in the place before Ilmorog was built (p. 3). The book itself was completed in October 1975, almost twelve years after Kenya's independence, the point at which the earlier novel stops. In *A Grain of Wheat* the struggle between the bourgeoisie and the peasants is still in its initial stages and is not expressed in explicit ideological terms, and whereas there is no mention of the role of the proletariat in the former novel, *Petals of Blood* takes us to a later period in both the history of Kenya and the development of Ngugi's social vision. Here the working class is asserting itself, and here Ngugi's partisan line is both explicit and unwavering.

In the first chapter of the novel we are introduced to the four main characters. Munira, Abdulla and Karega are all arrested in connection with the murder of three important persons. Wanja is in hospital after the burning of her house. The chapter ends with a newspaper report of the murders of the three African directors of Theng'eta Breweries, a capitalist company owned by an Anglo-American international combine. The murders are attributed to a so-called 'trade union agitator', a reference to Karega. We see straight away the idea of a struggle between international capitalism and the working class.

A few chapters later, a crucial event takes place: there is a severe drought and Ilmorog is threatened by famine. It is here that we begin to witness the leadership qualities of Karega, for it is he who initiates the idea of going to Nairobi to put Ilmorog's problem before the MP for the area, Nderi wa Riera. The importance of the journey is hinted at in the following words:

It was the journey, Munira was later to write, it was the exodus across the plains to the Big Big City that started me on that slow, almost ten-year, inward journey to a position where I can now see that man's estate is rotten at heart (pp. 117–18).

The author describes the journey as 'the exodus toward the kingdom of knowledge' (p. 118). What knowledge does the journey bring?

For the people of Ilmorog, the journey results in interesting revelations. In the first place, they are struck by the hypocrisy of organized (western-orientated) Christianity. An African minister, the Reverend Kamau, is so completely indoctrinated that he changes his name to 'the Reverend Jerrod Brown'. Munira, Karega and others take Joseph (who is sick) to this man of God, but all he can do for them is to pray ineffectually for the child (pp. 148-9). Jerrod Brown represents the theological arm of the rising bourgeoisie. Other representatives of this class include Chui, Kimeria and Nderi wa Riera. Chui was once a radical student at Siriana where he was expelled for leading a strike; now he has no time for the suffering peasants of Ilmorog. Kimeria was once Wanja's boyfriend. He now makes use of his status in society to force her to satisfy his sexual urge in the presence of elderly people well known to Wanja. Nderi wa Riera, the MP, has no interest in the people. Instead, he promotes the aims of the KCO (Kiama-Kamwene Cultural Organization), an organization whose objective is to divide the people and support the ruling class. The only exception is the kind lawyer, who, although part of the privileged few, devotes his life to the common good, a stand for which he pays heavily: in the end he is shot and killed.

The irony of the journey is that the people of Ilmorog went to Nairobi to invite capitalist forces which eventually deprive them of their land and means of production. Ilmorog develops into a typical urban centre and grows into a symbol of all urban centres in Kenya. These incidents give Ngugi the opportunity to criticize the spirit, ideology and life-styles of people in the upper echelons of capitalist society in Kenya. His criticism is aimed at three related forces: civilization, christianity and commerce. Capitalism is responsible not only for the poverty and misery of Abdulla and others, but also for the fact that Wanja becomes a prostitute. She is completely alienated from herself not just by selling her labour, but by selling her body as a commodity. For her life in Kenya has been reduced to the principle of the survival of the fittest. You exploit or you are exploited – 'You eat or you are eaten' (p. 293).

Theme and Para-linguistic Affective Devices

In *Petals of Blood* Ngugi's use of para-linguistic affective devices – symbols, illusions and other forms of indirect reference – is evident right from the beginning. On the page immediately preceding the Acknowledgements page, there is a reference to 'petals of blood'. Here, petals of blood are associated with a concealed but dangerous and poisonous serpent. On page 1 there is a passage from the sixth chapter of the New Testament Book of Revelation. Descriptions of horses and their fighting riders present images of violence and suppression to the reader's mind. Immediately below the Revelation passage is an extract from a poem by Walt Whitman. These lines present images of the violence of monarchical rulers against a people desirous of freeing themselves from oppression. We are also given a list of who in Ngugi's mind are obviously instruments of oppression – hangman, priest, tax-gatherer, soldier, jailer and so on. When we open the first chapter, we are immediately confronted with clear evidence of this violence and suppression. People are being arrested by policemen, and a murder has taken place.

A very important para-linguistic affective device is the symbol of the journey referred to above. For a fuller understanding of this, the reader must go beyond Chapter Six where the physical journey takes place and try to look comprehensively at the manner in which Ngugi employs the journey as a motif. Ngugi is not the only African writer who uses the journey motif to symbolize something larger than itself. It is also used in Sembène Ousmane's *God's Bits of Wood* and Ayi Kwei Armah's *Two Thousand Seasons*.[3] In *Petals of Blood* the journey operates at two levels. On one level there is the phsyical journey which takes place in Part Two, on the other, the whole book is conceived as a journey. This we can tell from the structure of the novel which is sub-divided into four parts as follows: Part One: *Walking*...(Chapters 1–6, pp. 1–118); Part Two: *Toward Bethlehem* pp. 119–87; Part Three: *To Be Born* (Chapters 7–10, pp. 189–259); Part Four: *Again*...*A Luta Continua!* (Chapters 11–13, pp. 261–345). The phrase *Walking Toward Bethlehem To Be Born Again* covers the entire book, which is consequently conceived as a journey toward Bethlehem for a rebirth. The closing slogan *A Luta Continua* means 'the struggle continues' and was used by some African liberation movements such as Frelimo of Mozambique and the Zimbabwe African National Union (ZANU) in their struggle for liberation.[4] To have a full grasp of the significance of the journey motif we must understand a number of things. First, Ngugi is here alluding to Yeats' poem, *The Second Coming*, which ends thus: 'And what rough beast, its hour come round at last, Slouches towards Bethlehem to be born?'[5]

Here Yeats is talking about the end of the Christian era and the coming of another era. The rough beast which slouches towards Bethlehem to be born symbolizes the advent of a new epoch which is to replace the Christian era. One possible interpretation is that Yeats was prophesying the coming of socialism, and that henceforth, socialist values were to replace Christian values just as Christian civilization had replaced Roman civilization in Europe. The poem was published a couple of years after the October Revolution of 1917 which established the first socialist government in the world. Yeats does refer to the Second Coming of Christ as described in St Matthew's Gospel (Chapter 24), and in *Petals of Blood* references to the Second Coming occur several times.

If for Yeats the Second Coming of Christ meant the advent of a new epoch, for Ngugi this rebirth has a multiplicity of meanings. Among other things it symbolizes the rebirth of Karega and Munira in their new visions of life, as we shall see later. But more importantly, walking towards Bethlehem to be born again are the people of Kenya. This is symbolized by the journey of the masses of Ilmorog to Nairobi. In Ngugi's mind Kenya is about to enter another struggle after which another republic will be born, i.e. a socialist republic. This interpretation is borne out by a number of events described in the book. First, the workers in Ilmorog are striking in support of Karega, 'the trade union agitator', and are now talking in terms of a movement of all the workers in Ilmorog (p. 343). Workers in other parts of the country, Nairobi – for instance – are also reported to be in action at the end of the book (p. 344). And lastly, there is now talk of another war of liberation (p. 344) As the girl Akinyi reports these things, Karega has a vision of a new Kenya:

> Tomorrow it would be the workers and the peasants leading the struggle and seizing power to overturn the system and all its prying, blood-thirsty gods and gnomic angels, bringing to an end the reign of the few over the many and the era of drinking blood and feasting on human flesh (p. 344).

According to Ngugi, therefore, the national struggle continues and victory is certain, hence *A Luta Continua!* This is socialist art, for socialist realism anticipates the future. As Ernst Fischer puts it, 'socialist art cannot content itself with blurred visions. Its task is, rather, to depict the birth of tomorrow out of today, with all the attendant problems.'[6]

Characterization: Karega's 'New Earth' and Munira's 'Petals of Blood'

The journey marks a turning point in the lives of the main characters – Munira, Karega, Abdulla and Wanja. For them it is more than a physical journey: it is a spiritual journey as well:

> For the journey had presented each with a set of questions for which there were no ready answers; had, because of what they had seen and experienced, thrown up challenges that could neither be forgotten nor put on one side, for they touched on things deep in the psyche, in their separate conceptions of what it meant to be human, a man, alive and free (p. 197).

After the journey both Munira and Karega undergo a profound transformation. In the first place, Munira begins to be jealous of Karega and to hate him. The hatred surfaces after Karega's confession which takes place during the Theng'eta drinking ceremony. Munira accuses Karega of driving his sister, Mukami, to her death and of mentioning her name in a dream in the same breath as 'a prostitute' – a reference to Wanja (pp. 239–49). In reality, however, Munira's motives are mixed here. His hatred is largely the outcome of Wanja's preference for Karega, for as she confesses to Munira later on, Karega has given back to her her sense of integrity as a woman (pp. 250–1).

From an ideological point of view, the differences between the two men become much clearer after the journey. Munira is converted by a charismatic Christian movement which is critical of what it sees as the hypocrisy and worldliness of the organized church, and preaches equality between the poor and the wealthy. The movement teaches its followers to scorn this world and fight for only one thing – the kingdom of God. Munira is 'born again' in a fanatical, evangelical way. On the other hand, Karega has a new social vision. On his return he announces his new vision to Wanja and Munira, the vision of a new world which must be created: 'Then we must create another world, a new earth' (p. 294). The new ideologist has been away from Ilmorog for five years and in the meantime he has worked as a trade unionist and is now committed to the destruction of capitalism and the construction of a socialist society:

> The true lesson of history was this: that the so-called victims, the poor, the down-trodden, the masses, had always struggled with spears and arrows, with their hands and songs of courage and hope to end their oppression and exploitation (p. 303).

Ngugi's treatment of Karega is a mark of his own understanding of a committed person's growth in ideological orientation and conscientization. Through theory and practice, through reading and working as a trade unionist, Karega is transformed from a mere radical nationalist to an ideologized representative of the proletariat. He even goes to the extent of disagreeing with the lawyer, his erstwhile mentor, for to Karega, the lawyer believes in the efficacy of parliamentary reforms, he worships 'the shrines of the monster'. As far as Karega is concerned, 'there must be another way . . . there must be another force that can be a match for the monster and its angels' (p. 288).

When we close the book we ask ourselves what Karega has achieved. He has helped to lead the workers of Ilmorog against the exploitation of a capitalist company, Theng'eta Breweries. He has been instrumental in raising the level of consciousness of the workers, in helping them to be fully aware of their exploitation and of the necessity to resist it. And what has Munira achieved? Obsessed with his idea of saving people from this vile world, Munira has gone to the extent of violence – murdering people. He sets Wanja's whorehouse on fire, his intention being to save Karega from Wanja's evil ways (motives mixed again here). However, it so happens that it is not Karega who is in Wanja's whorehouse at the time of the burning. Instead, there are the three compradors: the three African directors of Theng'eta Breweries – Chui, Mzigo, Kimeria. The fire Munira lights, the fire which swallows Wanja's house, forms a shape that looks like petals of blood: 'He stood on the hill and watched the whorehouse burn, the tongues of flame from the four corners forming petals of blood, making a twilight of the dark sky' (p. 333).

Thus the title *Petals of Blood* is directly associated with Munira. In other parts of the book we see the same association of petals of blood with this character. The expression 'petals of blood' is first used by one of his own schoolchildren to refer to a certain flower. Munira describes this flower with 'petals of blood' as a fruitless one: 'This is a worm-eaten flower', he says, 'It cannot bear fruit' (p. 22). Later on, our character himself uses the expression 'petals of blood' in the context of the murders he commits (p. 49). This takes us back to the very beginning of the novel where we are told about a serpent-like and dangerous flower. Munira is in fact a worm-eaten petal of blood: poisonous and incapable of bearing fruit. From his materialist standpoint, Ngugi depicts Munira's conversion as a kind of confused mysticism and religious idealism.

In *Petals of Blood*, Ngugi has portrayed 'typical characters in typical circumstances'. The distinction he makes between the lawyer who represents progressive elements in the upper echelons of society, forces describable as 'social democratic forces', and on the other hand Karega, the completely ideologized man, is most apt for there are such characters and differences in Kenya and other countries. Wanja and her prostitute employees are a familiar feature of some East African countries. Wanja is like Susi, the cunning prostitute in *After 4.30* of whom the typist says:

> Then nobody should say that Susi is wrong in doing what she does
> She is just as much of a prostitute as the world itself![7]

Ngugi gives us a sympathetic presentation of prostitutes: that they are what they are because social conditions have forced them to be so. Along with prostitutes must be considered the lumpen-proletariat. Ngugi gives us a typical example of this class in Abdulla. Capitalism has transformed Abdulla from a petty trader, a shopkeeper, to a member of the lumpen-proletariat. He becomes yet another example of those whom capitalism has exploited and impoverished.

But in the midst of all this poverty, this deprivation, there flourishes the national bourgeoisie – with examples like Chui, Mzigo and Kimeria. Difficult as it is to achieve within the space of one novel, Ngugi has attempted to depict as comprehensive a picture of post-independence Kenyan society as possible, to portray realistically the struggles and the forces at work in his society, and in so doing he has succeeded in capturing the mood of the epoch.

Ngugi's Approach to Literary Composition

From the point of view of narrative structure, *Petals of Blood* is a very complex novel, and this complexity is achieved through the use of several techniques. Among these is Ngugi's favourite technique – the flashback. At the beginning of Chapter One we meet the four major characters in their various situations after the murder of the three African directors of Theng'eta Breweries. We are also given a newspaper report of the murders. Thus chronologically the book opens towards the end of the story. At the beginning of the second chapter we go back to the beginning of the story, to the arrival of Munira in Ilmorog twelve years previously. The end of the chapter also marks the end of this flashback and Chapter Three brings us to the present where we meet Munira constructing a statement for the police. The flashback is combined with another technique, the 'confession', which occurs in Chapter Seven. Under the influence of Theng'eta, a local Kenyan brew, each person finds himself or herself giving an account of his secret past so that much is revealed about the personal history of Karega, Abdulla and Wanja.

Other techniques include the written report and the dream motif. Part of the story is told by Munira in the report he compiles for the police. This technique gives more insight to the motives and character of Munira. Dreams are also used to delve into the psyche of the characters. Thus Wanja, whose aunt died in a fire, often dreams about fire in a manner which clearly foreshadows the burning of her house. On the other hand, Karega, who is preoccupied with the revolution, has revolutionary dreams (pp. 234–8).

In narrative structure, *Petals of Blood* is more complex than *A Grain of Wheat*, but there are no passages which tax the reader as in the earlier novel. Linguistically, it is simpler as the following passage shows:

> The policeman came back and brought him a copy of the *Sunday Mouthpiece*. Munira simply looked at him: he was not any longer interested in reading. What did it matter whether one read or not? But he took the paper all the same and idly flipped through the pages. He sat up and stared at banner headlines of the fourth page. *Murder in Ilmorog. Foul play suspected. Political motivation?* The headline, as it turned out, was more dramatic than the story which followed. The news aspects of the incident would of course have been exhausted by the national dailies, especially the more sensational *Daily Mouthpiece*, Munira reflected, and hence the speculation without evidence. So that was the source of the policeman's theories (pp. 193–4).

In *Petals of Blood*, more than in any other novel he has written, Ngugi intersperses his narrative and descriptive passages with Swahili and Gikuyu words. The use of such words, while not reducing the readability of the novel in any significant way, nevertheless tends to hinder communication, or at least to irritate the reader. Here is an example:

> 'These children ... you have too much of the Foreigner's maneno maneno in your heads. Did you have a good gathano harvest in your place? Here it was poor and we don't know if the grains of maize and beans can last us to the end of the njahi rains. That is if the rains come ... ?

> 'I am not really a farmer,' Munira hastened to explain, all this talk of njahi, themithu, gathano and mwere, confusing him (pp. 8–9).

Or take the song which 'altered his (Munira's) life and outlook', but which loses its impact because the non-Swahili speaker does not understand it:

> Tukiacha dhambi, Mfalme mwema
> Hata tukifa, Tutatawala tena
> Halleluya, Halleluya
> Hata tukifa, Tutatawala tena (p. 296).

One major principle operating in the book is the synthesis of the local and the foreign, the old and the new. As in *A Grain of Wheat*, external references are an important aspect of the author's use of para-linguistic affective devices. Many of these external references are taken from the literatures of other nations. Ngugi borrows liberally from the Bible and from English literature. Thus we find quotations from the Book of Revelation and the Song of Solomon; from Walt Whitman, William Blake and William Butler Yeats, as has already been noted. These quotations are richly symbolic and are linked with the theme of the book. Thus the violence implicit in the quotation from the Book of Revelation highlights and underlines the themes of struggle and violence discussed in previous sections of this chapter. The verses from Blake and the Song of Solomon are all about love, sex and fertility, and they appear at the beginning of Part Three, which is devoted to fertility rituals, ending with the fruitful sexual relations between Wanja and Karega.

Whereas quotations from foreign literatures are used as external references, elements from traditional literature and culture in the form of songs, rhymes and legends are incorporated into the narrative. A typical example of traditional elements is the highly suggestive circumcision song sung during the circumcision dance (pp. 207-9). Also intermingled with these traditional elements are modern African songs. Some of these are highly political in content and Ngugi goes to the extent of quoting Amilcar Cabral, the late revolutionary leader of Guinea Bissau, and the nationalist slogan *A Luta Continua!*

The principle at work here is similar to that in Sembène Ousmane's *God's Bits of Wood*, as we explained in Chapter Seven. With Ngugi the fusion of local and foreign elements is a clear indication of the writer's socialist approach to literary composition. In this respect, Ngugi's approach is very different from that of Achebe. Achebe is, from a Marxist point of view, narrowly nationalistic, for in *Arrow of God* he enriches his narrative with literary and cultural elements from Igbo society only, whereas Ngugi accepts whatever is of literary value from other cultures, while uplifting his own cultural heritage. Writing in *Social Sciences*, Mikhail Khrapchenko has said, 'socialist literature and art do not stand aloof from the development of art in other countries and accept all that is progressive and valuable that has been created by great artists from other countries'.[8] It has also been said that a progressive artist 'while remaining a son of his own people' does not scorn the achievements of other people and that 'progressive art serves simultaneously the interests of its own people and of mankind, its own time and the future'.[9] This requirement of socialist art is clearly fulfilled in Ngugi's greatest novels, *Petals of Blood* and *A Grain of Wheat*. While he is obviously partisan in his political views, in his support for the proletariat in its struggle against the bourgeoisie, Ngugi does not hesitate to incorporate elements from western bourgeois art in his own composition; while he is obviously materialistic in his approach to religion, as is demonstrated by his treatment of Munira's religious fanaticism, he does not hesitate to enrich his work with quotations from the Christian Bible.

A significant feature of Ngugi's technique and style is realism. In his descriptive passages he is not merely naturalistic, simply reproducing photographic representations of reality with abstract and detached objectivity. Instead he sees the connection between the individual and the general, the 'typical' and the 'particular' in the Lukács sense. The school in Ilmorog is described as barren and lifeless, and is in that respect indistinguishable from its surroundings. This is a reflection of the whole Ilmorog region, for Ilmorog is a dry unproductive place, an arid 'waste land', as one police officer describes it (p. 2).

Ngugi's realism is also seen in his attempt to capture the totality of life at this particular time and phase of history. When he describes the harvest season in a year of plenty in Chapter Seven he does not restrict himself to the activities of people. Instead he depicts man, the land, animals, plants – in short man and nature – interacting and celebrating in one festive mood at this time of universal productivity. This, for instance, is a passage typifying this festive mood:

> There was something about harvesting, whether it was maize or beans or peas, which always released a youthful spirit in everyone. Children ran about the fields to the voices of women raised to various pitches of despairing admonition about the trails of waste. Sometimes the children surprised a hare or an antelope in a lair among the ripened crops: they would quickly abandon whatever they were carrying and run after the animal the whole length of Ilmorog, shouting: Kaaau...Kaaau...catch...catch it...catch meat. Even old men looked like children, in their eyes turned to the fields: only they tried to hide their trembling excitement as they carried token sheaves of beans to the threshing-ground. ... Women winnowing beans in the wind was itself a sight to see: sometimes the breeze would stop and women would curse and wait holding their wicker trays ready to catch the breeze when it returned. ... Later it was the turn of the cows: they were left loose to roam through the harvested fields of maize: they would run about, tails held up to the sky, kicking up dust with their hind legs, their tongues reaching out for the standing feed of maize. Sometimes the male would run after a young female giving it no rest or time to eat, expecting another kind of harvest (pp. 203–4).

It has been said that a 'realistic' work 'is rich in a complex, comprehensive set of relations between man, nature and history'.[9] Nothing demonstrates this statement better than the passage just quoted. Here Ngugi attempts to relate each individual, each type of creature, to the social whole. Nothing is seen in isolation from other things. The festive mood of the creatures depicted here is in turn linked to the circumcision ceremony which is a key element of the fertility rituals celebrated in the novel (pp. 206–11). The circumcision dance and the song have heavy sexual connotations. Sex is an important motif for Ngugi, since it is a symbol of fertility, productivity and life. Karega's sexual contact with Wanja is a fruitful exercise (pp. 229–31) because it brings back Wanja's womanhood, it brings back life to Wanja who has for many years been overwhelmed by the fear of being barren. The fact that Karega succeeds in rousing sexual feelings in Wanja when, despite his long relationship with her, Munira fails to do so (p. 251) is symbolic of Karega's productivity and Munira's failure in life.

Conclusion

It is clear that when he wrote *Petals of Blood*, Ngugi firmly believed in the socialist revolution and was deeply aware of the nature of the class struggle in the new state of Kenya. Ngugi is committed to the cause of the workers and peasants.

But if in *Petals of Blood* Ngugi is a committed socialist, is he a pamphleteer who uses the artistic form of the novel merely to promote socialist propaganda? Are his characters invented for the sole purpose of driving home a political point? Does Ngugi feel a strong desire to take a public stand to testify to his convictions 'before the entire world'?[10] There are indeed cases when Ngugi's political argument becomes too overt, as, for example, when he uses such common political slogans as *A Luta Continua* and when he projects his ideological views in Karega's words, dreams and communications with the revolutionary lawyer. Coupled with this are certain artistic flaws. For one thing there is too much coincidence in the book. Why is it that when the marchers from Ilmorog are looking for help in Nairobi, they happen to come to the houses of Chui, Kimeria and Kamau? The coincidence borders on the implausible.[11] The book is also unnecessarily wordy at times. The economy and tautness of *A Grain of Wheat* is gone and our writer is tempted to be prolific in style. But that said, the novel's complexity of narrative structure, the diversity and richness of character displayed in Karega, Munira, Wanja and Abdulla, the rich and sophisticated symbolism, the depth of social awareness evident throughout the narrative – these are qualities that make *Petals of Blood* a superb work of art. From an ideological standpoint, Ngugi's novel is socialist art *par excellence*, for 'it expresses the thoughts, feelings, moods, points of view and hopes of the new epoch and of its new class'.[12] We can therefore conclude that *Petals of Blood* is a very successful blend of artistic excellence and ideological clarity.

Notes

1 *Petals of Blood*, London, Heinemann African Writers Series 188, 1977.
2 *A Grain of Wheat*, London, Heinemann African Writers Series 36, 1967.
3 In *God's Bits of Wood* the march of the women to Dakar closely resembles the journey of the people of Ilmorog to Nairobi.
4 This appears incorrectly in some editions as *La Luta Continua!*
5 W. B. Yeats, The Second Coming,
6 Ernst Fischer, *The Necessity of Art: A Marxist Approach*, p. 112.
7 *After 4.30*, p. 82.

8 USSR Academy of Sciences, *Social Sciences*, Vol. 3, 1979, p. 102.
9 Eagleton, *Marxism and Literary Criticism*, p. 28.
10 See Engels to Minna Kautsky, *On Literature and Art*, p. 88.
11 For this point I am indebted to Professor D. A. Tuohy of the National University of Lesotho.
12 Ernst Fischer, *The Necessity of Art*, p.180.

9 *The Price of Commitment: La Guma's* In the Fog of the Seasons' End

Theme

In the Fog of the Seasons' End[1] tells the story of Beukes, a working-class South African Coloured, Elias Tekwane, a proletarian with a peasant background, and Isaac, a factory worker who does not feature prominently in the narrative. The novel focuses on the activities of an underground movement which these three characters work for, Elias Tekwane being the commander of the section to which they all belong. On the other side of the coin there is the police force, characterized by violent reactions to the movement, and the agitation of the proletariat. The underground movement and the police can therefore be seen as two antagonistic forces opposing each other and competing for the control of society.

South Africa is portrayed as a police state, and the activities of the police are the physical manifestation of the harsh realities of apartheid South Africa. We see this in the inhuman treatment of the prisoner in the prologue – a treatment that foreshadows the torture of Elias Tekwane at the end of the book. It is evident in the harassment of innocent people in Chapter Five, when police road blocks are set up and working-class people are arrested for little or no reason. And when the masses stage a strike in which they attempt to reject one of the symbols of their bondage and oppression – the pass – the police resort to the unquestionable authority of the gun (pp. 104–5).

It is such conditions as these which force lovers of freedom to operate underground. The underground movement is part of a larger nationalist struggle which the officials and the mass media are hiding from the public. The papers flash the proceedings in the trial of a murderess but the guerrilla incursions are only reported in a 'side column' where the Minister of Police announces: 'The Republic is facing a new wave of guerrilla incursions on its northern borders.... African nationalist infiltrators are stirring up the local population' (p. 62). The quiet tone of the narrative is a reflection of the manner in which the organization operates. Its agents have to move quietly, carefully, avoiding police barriers, contacting those who are sympathetic, spreading propaganda under cover of darkness, and recruiting men to go and join the ranks of guerrilla trainees. The conditions under which the movement operates are summarized in Chapter Four:

The movement writhed under the terror, bleeding. It had not been defeated, but it had been beaten down. It crouched like a slugged boxer, shaking his spinning head to clear it, while he took the count, waiting to rise before the final ten. Life still throbbed in its aching arms and fingers; wholesale arrests had battered it. The leaders and the cadres filled the prisons or retreated into exile. Behind them, all over the country, tiny groups and individuals who had escaped the net still moved like moles underground trying to link up in the darkness of lost communications, and broken contacts (p. 48).

The movement is also concerned with the political education of the young (p. 88), which is necessary in the face of an education system which is calculated to mystify, a system which is designed to 'befog the mind' (p. 86). To do this, the movement has to rely on progressive teachers like Flotman, who risk undoing the harm done by the education system.

La Guma also shows how organizations of this nature have to push forward in spite of spies. Oppressive regimes always establish a network of spies not only to get information about the revolution, but also to strike fear into the hearts of those sympathetic to it. Some will be prevented from participating in the struggle by the sheer force of the oppressor's psychological hold on the mind. But to Beukes the struggle must go on regardless: 'We have to risk talking to people', he says, for 'If we worry too much about spies we'll get nothing done' (p. 96). This is part and parcel of Beukes' courage and optimism which astounds Flotman:

Flotman said, 'Tchah. But I admire the way you boggers go ahead. Nothing seems to stop you. What drives you?'

'Drives? Nothing drives us,' Beukes replied. 'We understand our work, so we enjoy it. It is rarely that one is happy in one's work.'

'You go to jail, you get beaten up by the fascist police. All right, all right, no lecture is required. But Jesus Christ, don't you baskets ever get fed up?' (p. 87).

But La Guma, as a writer concerned to reflect 'the realities of South Africa'[2] is not satisfied in portraying the activities of the underground movement and those of the police in the abstract. The activities of the forces of progress and reaction must be depicted in the context of specific historical conditions. La Guma therefore gives us a glimpse of the conditions and relations of production which give rise to the social unrest and the resultant police repression, for just as the agitation of the masses is the outcome of relations of production, police brutality can only be the physical manifestation of an ideology which, when challenged, resorts to the use of force. The relations of production in South Africa, as in other exploitative societies, are relations of exploitation, domination and subordination.[3] An example of the relations of exploitation prevalent in South Africa are the inadequate transport facilities provided for the black workers. The stampede and bustle in buses described in Chapter Five (pp. 68–9) is clear evidence of the exploitation of the Coloured and African worker by capitalist forces in South Africa. The bus company is only interested in profit, not in the comfort of the passengers who pay money to ride the buses – hence the provision of buses which are so few that the workers are packed like sardines and have to compete savagely for seats. The workers themselves are aware of their exploitation, and so one of them can't help bursting out, 'F . . . the company, f . . . the bosses. They just making f . . . ing money out of us poor people' (p. 69). Another example of exploitation is the record of miners who sacrifice their lives in the bowels of the earth in the process of production and either lose their lives completely or go back home horribly disfigured and deformed by disease, unable even to bring sweets to their children (p. 132).

A typical example of subordination are the regulations governing the lives of Africans in urban areas. As the author puts it, when Africans turn sixteen they are 'born again', they are 'confirmed into the blood rites of a servitude as cruel as Caligula, as merciless as Nero', a servitude whose bonds are 'the tangled chains of infinite regulations' (p. 80), regulations which determine who an African worker is, where he comes from, where he is allowed to work, where he may not go, etc. So absolute is the power of the Bantu Commissioner over the African that he can quote the authority of the law to say the following – and mean what he says:

> 'If these things are not followed with care, then into the prison with you or all permits cancelled so that you cease to exist. You will be nothing, nobody, in fact you will be decreated. You will not be able to go anywhere on the face of this earth, no man will be able to give you work, nowhere will you be able to be recognized; you will not eat or drink; you will be as nothing, perhaps even less than nothing.' (p. 82)

The effect of pronouncements of this nature is to reduce the African worker to the status of a slave, and La Guma enables the reader to see how characters like Elias Tekwane are the direct result of such a deplorable state of affairs. Elias' father was killed in a mining accident, and the compensation that his mother received after the accident amounted to peanuts compared to what White widows had. (p. 47). Elias himself is subjected to the inhumanity of the Bantu Commissioner's authority. Among other things, he is not given the freedom to give his own age as he knows it. White clerks and their Black assistants know better. They can tell his 'right age' by pulling down his trousers and examining his pubic hair, an example of how blacks are subjected to one of the basest forms of human indignity and humiliation (pp. 126–7).

It is under conditions such as these that we see the proletariat growing in consciousness and uniting to revolt against one of the most dehumanizing regulations – the pass law. This is a brave act of defiance, the expression of something much greater than the forced holding of passes. All of the working class unite in their determination to dump the passes at the police station:

There were elderly people, and children who had boycotted the schools that day; workers who had stayed away from the Steel Town, to show that they were tired of regimentation and chattels, of bullying police and arrogant foremen, of fines and taxes and having too little money with which to buy food. There were women, singing and swaying in the shade of umbrellas, and young girls giggling under the eyes of youths who strutted in black berets, patched trousers and ragged shirts. (p. 102)

The strike, which is not the only one recorded in the book, is an instance of the continual agitation of the masses aimed at shaking the power of the ruling classes.[4] La Guma's portrayal of this particular strike is so accurate and detailed that he will not omit the mention of members of the lumpen-proletariat – here represented by the Outlaw – for the lumpen-proletariat, i.e. beggars, prostitutes, thieves and other people of no definite occupation who have sunk to the lower depth of society, are the natural consequence of the capitalist mode of production. While the workers are motivated by the desire to break the chains of slavery, the Outlaw's motive in joining the crowd is to pick pockets and pilfer (p. 103).

Apart from giving us an insight into the conditions under which the exploited Blacks live, the author also attempts to show us something of the life-styles of White bourgeois society. La Guma is not very successful here because the picture he gives is inadequate, but he provides us with 'windows' through which we can get a glimpse of White bourgeois society. The first of these 'windows' is the factory where Isaac works (pp. 110 ff). Here we meet White typists chattering about marriages and reading about the murderess who killed her husband, quite unaware of the greater threat to their security posed by the Blacks who work under them (pp. 115–16). We also see in this chapter a familiar feature of race relations in apartheid South Africa. To White people all African males, whether young, middle-aged or old men, are simply 'boys'. So the typists refer to Isaac and his fellow workers as 'boys'. What is more, these 'boys' do not exist as people in the minds of the privileged whites. They were 'only noticeable when an order had to be given or when a favour was required' (p. 111). The other 'window' is the occasion when, running away from the police, Beukes wanders into an upper-class White suburb where 'rich white folk (were) having themselves a Friday-night do' – theirs is a life of parties and pleasure as opposed to the misery, humiliation, and violent oppression which characterizes the life of the poor and oppressed Blacks (p. 148). In depicting scenes from these various sections of South African society La Guma is, in his limited way, trying to present a total picture of how men live out their roles in this class and oppressive society.

Language, Character and Social Class

La Guma is a South African 'Coloured' and, unlike Ngugi or Achebe, has the advantage of using English as a mother tongue. He is familiar with the idiom of

Coloured, Afrikaaners and, evidently, African speakers of English. Here is a typical example of low-class 'Coloured English' as spoken by Isaac and the other 'boys':

> '*Hoezit, boeta* Ike?' he said, 'What do you say today then?'
>
> 'Hullo, Sam,' Isaac said. Then, to the old woman, 'Any chance of getting a cup of tea, ahead of all the Great White Fathers?'
>
> 'You got to pour it yourself,' the old woman said, wiping sweat from her fallen chin. 'Is like an oven in here.'
>
> 'Blerry warm outside too,' Sam said with his mouth full of polony and bread...
>
> 'You should ask them to get you a scooter,' Isaac said, pouring tea. 'And since you're on the rounds, you better not let *ou* Queen Mother in front catch you, hey. She got a hangover like three sailors and she is crying for Alka-Seltzer, so you might have to leave all the company's business to save her head.'
>
> 'I'd like to give her a dose of Epsom Salts,' Sam said. 'Ike, you going to sit by the *klaberjas* game lunchtime?'
>
> 'Hell,' Isaac said, sitting down. 'Is that all you boggers do lunchtime? To play cards?'
>
> 'Ah, Ikey *ou* pa,' Sam said, stirring his tea. 'You could *mos* take us all down to the square in the old days to hear a meeting. Nowadays all meetings is *mos* stopped, don't I say? All you can hear now is them holy rollers. There's *mos* nothing else to do. Now we know *mos* you a good *klaberjas* player, pally, and I need a partner.' (pp. 113–14)

And the following passage is a reflection of the modes of speech of the uneducated Afrikaaner policeman:

> 'F... you. Who in the blerry hell do you think you are? Let me see what you got in that parcel.'
>
> 'Just my overalls, *meneer*, just my overalls. Taking them home to be washed.'
>
> 'Open up, you hell, before I *donder* you.'
>
> 'Hey, what the hell goes on there in front? A man must *mos* get home for supper.'
>
> 'Jesus, working, all day and now there is this hold up.'
>
> '*Jong, waar's jou pas*? Where's your pass?'
>
> Pale white fingers like maggots flicked over the pages, identifying the bearer against the photograph. 'Lord, all you *bliksems* look the blerry same. Where did your mother get you from, hey?' The pages rustled one over the other, 'Hey, hey, you did not pay your tax this year, hey?'
>
> 'I paid the poll tax months ago.'
>
> 'Like blerry hell you did. Come along, boy, come along.'
>
> 'I paid.'

'F . . . you. You think I'm a bloody baboon? And don't give me your bloody cheek either. Here, constable take this one to the van.'

'But if you look you will see the stamp.'

'Listen to me, *bliksem*, do you think I have got time to waste? Think you I have got all night to listen to you? You can tell it all to the magistrate *bass*.'

'*Jong*, come along, jump, jump.'

'Jong, kom, kom, kom, pas, man, pas.'

'What the f . . . ing hell you got in that pocket. *Dagga*, hey? You bastards live on that f . . . ing weed, I reckon.'

'It's only my tobacco.' (p. 67)

The English of the Afrikaaner policeman is thus full of vulgar words, insulting words and words of Afrikaans origin. It is characterized by such words as *blerry*, *fuck*, '*bliksems*', *baboon*, *bloody*. It is a language that reflects not only the linguistic background of the policeman, but also his social habits – he is unpolished and unrefined – as well as the racial prejudices of the society. Africans are '*bliksems*', *baboons* and *bastards*. The tenor of discourse is a clear indication of the relations of domination and subordination that characterize the South African social scene. The White policeman has no obligation to be polite to the subordinate Blacks. His is a voice of harsh command all the time, while the Blacks have to use such words of respect as *Meneer* 'Mr' and *bass* 'boss'.

Beukes seems to alter his style of speaking slightly depending on the inter-locutor. Thus in the company of people like Erny or Tommy, his conversational style is more colloquial, whereas when talking to Elias who speaks in a more standard fashion, his English is more 'refined' and sounds like standard English. Here is Beukes talking to Erny:

Beukes moved off into the crowd, aimlessly, still trying to decide whether to invest his money at the booths. Suddenly a voice cried out loudly, 'Hey, *ou* Buke, hey, what the hell you doing here, hey?'

He looked at the man who had shouted and smiled, 'Hullo, old Erny, howzit? Same thing you doing, I reckon.'

Erny cried, 'Long time no see. I lost fifteen bob on these games, man. It's a swindle. You reckon I'm a sucker? The only time you get your money's worth is on the swings and the big wheel and stuff like that. I took these goosies on the big wheel and they carried on like they was being murdered or something!'

Beukes looked at the two girls with Erny and said, 'Hullo there.' (p. 36)

And here is Beukes discussing serious matters with Elias:

Elias nodded seriously then went on. 'First, I was to tell you that there are three men who have to be taken north and across the border. They are going to be trained for the military wing. Since you are in charge of transport for the first stage of the trip from here, you should arrange for your man to take them.

They will meet on Monday at the usual place for such things.'

'Will I know them?' Beukes asked.

'I don't know,' Elias answered, puffing at his pipe. 'But they will be named Peter, Paul and Michael.' He laughed through the drifting grey smoke. 'We are making use of the saints. Perhaps I should not be Hazel. There is no Saint Hazel, is there?'

'Not that I have heard of,' Beukes smiled. 'Saint Hazel, hey? If there were four of us we could be Matthew, Mark, Luke and John.' Somewhere out in the dark the dog yapped again and the siren of a train wailed distantly.

'Well,' Elias said. 'Michael, Peter and Paul then, and you will see that they get away all right, yes?'

'Of course,' Beukes said and dropped the end of his cigarette in a saucer which served as an ashtray. The lamp flickered faultily and he looked at it for a moment. He said, 'It is a good thing that we are now working for armed struggle. It gives people confidence to think that soon they might combine mass activity with military force. One does not like facing the fascist guns like sheep.' It was like a slogan. (p. 143)

La Guma is obviously not concerned with language variation as a reflection of the idiosyncracies of individual speakers! The only example of a peculiarly individual style of speech is that of the flamboyant clown, Tommy, whose English is marked by the rhythm and poetry of jazz music. In all other cases La Guma displays language variation to reveal the speech habits of a social group. In this regard, two social groups stand out as having marked dialectical characteristics: low-class Coloureds and the uneducated Afrikaaner policeman. The speech habits of these two groups also seem to resemble each other probably because Coloured English is influenced by Afrikaans. The author is right in attributing a formal style of speech to Elias Tekwane because the majority of good African speakers of English learn the language in the formal situation of the classroom and from books, and do not use the colloquial style of Coloureds or Black Americans. Elias is therefore typically African in his manner of speech.

Just as language variation is more a reflection of social class and status than a mark of individual speech habits, La Guma's characters tend to be 'types' rather than individuals. There is the music-loving Casanova, Tommy, a symbol of the apolitical but useful type; there is Flotman, the ideologized school teacher; there is Bennett, the frightened sympathizer; there is Isaac, the politically-conscious worker who eventually joins the liberation forces in the bush – all these types exist in real life. As for the policemen, they are only 'typical' representations of instruments of oppression in that oppressive society – they possess no individuality. The only developed characters are Elias and Beukes, and even they cannot match the 'roundness' of Ousmane's Bakayoko or Ngugi's three main characters – Munira, Karega and Wanja.

In his descriptive and narrative passages La Guma uses Standard English. The style, which can be quite difficult to follow, is neatly controlled. There are no unnecessary emotional outbursts, and the writer's own description of representatives of the various sections of the population is free of prejudice. And yet, in its controlled manner La Guma's prose can accurately depict a moment of intense activity, quick action, confusion and bewilderment. Here is a passage where he describes the police shootings and the reaction of the masses during 'the big strike':

> Then for some reason or another, a policeman shot into the noise. The sound of the shot was almost lost under the chanting, the singing, the laughter. Silence dropped from the gaping mouths of those who saw and heard, gaping in sudden wonder. Then there was a thin wailing and the front turned, the crowd surged back. Then all the police began to fire, a ragged volley at first. The crowd was already bursting away, scattering wide, a jumbled, falling, headlong rush away from the smoking iron muzzles of the guns; a wide-eyed fear, bewilderment, incongruous laughter from those who thought these were only warning shots. The firing burst out again like a roll of metal-skinned drums. From the front of the Police Station, from the groups around the trucks, from the turret of the armoured car, the shiny brass cylinders of spent ammunition leaped and cascaded for a moment in deadly ejaculations, and then stopped. (p. 104)

This is probably an artistic recreation of the shootings at Sharpeville and Langa in 1960, so that La Guma is using actual historical facts to lend his narrative an atmosphere of urgency and immediacy. Note how the author's graphic description recreates the atmosphere of a climax to an episode, how the author attempts to portray the movement of the great mass of people, the rhythm of the police guns, the pandemonium and confused reaction of the masses – a mixture of singing and laughter turning into gaping, wailing bewilderment and 'wide-eyed fear'. And note how, in the passage below, the author manages to portray the prevailing atmosphere of a heavy silence in the vicinity immediately after the police shootings. This is an accurate depiction, in minute detail, of the finality of the police shootings, the unquestionable authority of the gun over the defenceless masses:

> With the end of the volley came a silence of finality. Even the dogs of the Township did not bark. In the open field, in the dusty alleyways where they had tried to flee, the dead and the dying now lay like driftwood. The silence lay heavy and awkward for a while, until the wounded began to cry out for help. Then the stunned people drifted anxiously back to touch the dead and comfort the maimed. (p. 104)

And although he avoids a shouting tone, La Guma does not want to distort, thereby, the experiences of those who fell victim to the cruelty of the gun. He can make the reader see and feel the wrenching of flesh, the breaking of bones and the vulnerability of the body which suddenly became evident in that one moment of police action. This is how he describes the death of the Bicycle Messenger:

> The Bicycle Messenger had died instantly, sprawled jointlessly over his fallen cycle which he had refused to abandon in flight, his flesh burst open, his spine shattered and his splintered ribs thrust into heart and lungs. One of his ankle clips had come off and was entangled in the spokes of a wheel. (p. 105)

This is the harsh violence alluded to in the poem quoted at the beginning of the book (opposite page 1). These are the 'fragile and fugitive' martyrs who are butchered by the enemy at the height of the struggle before the final victory, the martyrs whose 'black entrails' are 'shattered like the spider's web' 'in the fog of the seasons' end' – at the beginning of the end of the exploitation of man by man in South Africa.

In the Bicycle Messenger passage, La Guma describes the condition of a dead person who can no longer feel what we feel or see the horror that we see. But La Guma can also reflect, in an amazing manner, the experience of pain, showing how it feels to be in pain. In the following passage he portrays the torture to which Elias Tekwane is subjected by the police. The passage reflects not only the physical pain that Elias experiences, but also the psychological war he has to fight within himself. He is determined to resist the temptation to betray his comrades even if it means dying a painful death, but the desire to save oneself and sacrifice the cause, the struggle, is irresistibly there. So Tekwane's torture is two-pronged – it is physical and psychological, and is told in magnificent and powerful poetic prose:

> Elias screamed. He had anticipated the violence, but not this, not this. Talk, talk, talk, his mind told him while his body jerked and jigged like a broken puppet on badly-manipulated strings. But far, far away the ghosts gathered, the feathers bobbed and swayed, the leopard tails swung, and the sun, like a yellow lantern in the resistant sky, glanced like lightning from the hammered spearblades.
>
> His flesh burned and scorched and his limbs jerked and twitched and fell away from him, jolting and leaping in some fantastic dance which only horror linked to him. A thousand worms writhed under his skin and broke through the surface of his flesh, each one of them shrieking in the black darkness, while far away the ghosts drifted along the hazy horizon and beckoned to him to come to join them. (p. 173)

Narrative Technique and the Articulation of Socialist Ideology

Alex La Guma employs the omniscient narrator technique which gives him, as author and narrator, the freedom to explore the inner thoughts and psychological experiences of his characters, particularly the main ones, Beukes and Elias. This is how he depicts the psychological and physical agony Elias goes through at the end of the book. The first person narrator point of view would not be appropriate here, particularly as Elias is clearly going to die in the private world of a cell and cannot tell his tale in person to the living.

Another important feature of our author's narrative technique is the use of the flashback. By shifting the focus from the present to the past of his characters and vice versa, La Guma is able to give us a clear picture of the background and social circumstances surrounding the lives of Beukes and Elias. This is how we get to know about Beukes' love affair with Frances and their eventual marriage. This is how we get to know Elias' social and family background. Sometimes the flashback takes the form of remembered memories from the past. La Guma can gently take the reader by the hand to the past in a character's dream world and then suddenly bring him back to the present. The following passage shows how we are told about Beukes' first visit to Frances' home. Beukes is taken up by the memory of his second encounter with Frances while sitting in Abdullah's house, so that he momentarily forgets about the present. All of a sudden he becomes aware of the fact that he is sitting in Abdullah's house with Abdullah's mother who is sewing:

> Then out of a short stretch of passageway had come Frances. She had a towel wrapped around her head and there had been soapsuds on her brown arms, and the young man had noticed with surprise how long-legged she was and how her small breasts had pulled up under the overall she wore, as she had rubbed her hair with the towel. There had been a knotted feeling in his stomach as he had come out of the chair, smiling.
>
> She had wrinkled her nose at him and had said, 'There, I told you if you came too early I'd still be washing my hair.'
>
> He had said, loving her, 'Well, at least I can see you with your paint off, too.'
>
> Suddenly he was aware that the woman at the sewing-machine had stopped chattering, and looking at her he saw her kerchiefed head cocked, listening. Footsteps grated outside, then the front door rattled and there was somebody in the hallway. (p. 94)

The 'She' in the greater part of the passage refers to Frances and therefore belongs to Beukes' dream-world, while 'the woman at the sewing-machine' is a reference to Abdullah's mother. The switch from the past to the present is indicated by the clause 'suddenly he was aware'. And by the time the reader is brought back to the present, he has been given information which he would otherwise not have had. This kind of technique is exploited in Ngugi's *A Grain of Wheat*.

The flashback is also used to link chapters. At the end of a chapter, La Guma not infrequently introduces an idea relating to something that happened in the past, and then in the next chapter we see the past event being described in full. For example, Chapter Five ends with Beukes thinking about his meeting with

Hazel, and the next chapter opens with the sentence 'Hazel was the code name for Elias Tekwane', and in this chapter the story of Elias' early life is narrated. Similarly, at the end of Chapter Eight Beukes and Abdullah are discussing the time of 'the big strike' and the next chapter is all about the strike. In this way, La Guma's chapters flow naturally and logically into each other.

Another important aspect of La Guma's narrative technique is the implicit expression of optimism that runs through the book: the idea that however difficult the struggle may be, victory is certain. This idea no doubt derives from the materialist view of history – that history is on the side of the proletariat. So whatever form of struggle the proletariat is engaged in helps to propel history forward. The idea is most explicitly expressed in Beukes' optimism which, as mentioned above, strikes people like Flotman as unusual (p. 87). It is also demonstrated in the successes of the underground movement. The success of the movement is reflected in the coverage given to it in the news media. This is the significance of the newspaper which Beukes leaves in the park to be picked up by Beatie Adams. The story of a woman who murdered her husband catches the headlines: 'A woman accused of murdering her husband was to appear in court that morning: Bainsburg murder, Woman appears Today, the headline stated.' (p. 13) The case is also flashed in the morning paper on the day Isaac disappears from the factory where he worked and is one of the major subjects of discussion among the White typists (pp. 115–16). But after the movement has done its work, the story of the murderess is completely overshadowed by the success of the organization's campaign:

> Beukes had already read the reports with some astonishment. The headlines splashed in black, astounded letters: 'Explosions scatter pamphlets . . . Leaflet bombs hit the city . . . Underground movement still active.' The woman who had murdered her husband had been relegated to an inside page. (p. 144)

Even the appearance of a crushing defeat for the masses is not seen as totally negative, for every step taken by the proletariat to shake the capitalist exploiters and their oppressive state machinery is a step forward. Any defeat can only constitute a momentary setback. Thus the masses are massacred on the day of 'the big strike' and the attempt to dump the passes at the police station ends in disaster, but after the massacres there is a downpour of rain which mingles with the blood of the martyrs – a symbol of the fruitfulness of the struggle:

> While the living wandered, some aimlessly and others with purpose, among the dead and dying and wounded, the sky muttered darkly at last and started to shed heavy drops of rain. Thunder clashed along the horizon like a duel of artillery and then the rain began to fall steadily to mingle with the blood. (p. 105)

The fact that these words occur at the end of the chapter and constitute the epilogue to the author's narration of the strike event is not merely fortuitous.

The author employs this para-linguistic affective device of fruitfulness at the end of the chapter to highlight the theme of optimism, to dispel all feelings of despair.

Of course the progress of the revolution has to be seen in terms of a dialectic between action and reaction, victory and defeat. Consequently, soon after the movement has scored major successes and managed to gain maximum publicity, Beukes is badly wounded and Elias is finally caught – the forces of reaction are also making progress. But, like the death of the strikers, Elias' death is not seen as a symbol of failure on the part of the masses. La Guma is realistic in that he does not shy away from portraying truthfully the power of the oppressors over the struggling masses. It is true that many revolutionaries are caught and tortured to death. One only needs to remember Steve Biko who died in prison and Mahlangu who was hanged for his part in the struggle. These are the realities of the South African situation which La Guma seeks to expose in his novel. So Elias, the leader of a unit of the underground movement, is caught and tortured to death by electrocution. But such a death does not engender despair for, as Lenin said, despair is alien to the working-class movement: 'Despair is characteristic of moribund classes', but the proletariat 'is not one of these classes'.[5] When he is dying Elias sees a vision of his ancestors rising in resistance and coming to his aid (pp. 173–5). And to articulate further his optimism in artistic form, the author does not close the book with an account of Elias' death. In the final chapter we see three recruits being sent to the north to be trained in the techniques of guerrilla warfare. For La Guma, this is the resolution to the problem. The internal struggle merges with the externally-based armed liberation struggle, and herein lies the answer to the situation. The armed ancestors whom Elias sees in his hour of death will indeed come to fight, but in the form of guerrillas armed with modern weapons.

The sun that rises in the east is a symbol of a new dawn in the history of South Africa. It is La Guma's way of expressing the victory that comes from the east, the victory of the socialist revolution. The sun 'brightening the east' heralds the coming of a new day, the beginning of a mighty revolution which is the natural consequence of the apartheid rule in South Africa. It is capitalism and its oppressive state machinery that have produced the likes of Hazel and Beukes. The same thing has given rise to the militant consciousness of Peter, Paul and Michael. But the recruitment of Peter, Paul and Michael is only the tip of an iceberg, one single manifestation of the mighty revolution which is to come and sweep away the present exploitative system, whose perpetrators are now warned to take heed. These ideas are all embodied in the second and third last paragraphs of the novel, which are immensely optimistic in tone:

The sun was brightening the east, now, clearing the roofs of the suburb and the new light broke the shadows into scattered shapes. Henny April waved again, and Beukes watched the old van turn into the street and then it was wheeling away between the soiled houses, the scanty garden-lots, leaving behind a mist of blue smoke.

Beukes stood by the side of the street in the early morning and thought, they have gone to war in the name of a suffering people. What the enemy himself has created, these will become battle-grounds, and what we see now is only the tip of an iceberg of resentment against an ignoble regime, the tortured victims of hatred and humiliation. And those who persist in hatred and humiliation must prepare. Let them prepare hard and fast – they do not have long to wait. (pp. 180–1)

Notes

1 *In the Fog of the Season' End*, London, Heinemann African Writers Series 110, 1972.
2 Hans Zell and H. Silver, *A Reader's Guide to African Literature*, p. 149.
3 *The Fundamentals of Marxist-Leninist Philosophy*, Progress Publishers, p. 354.
4 See E. Fischer, *Marx in His Own Words*, p. 88.
5 See V.I. Lenin, 'Articles on Tolstoy,' in D. Craig (ed.), *Marxists on Literature*, p. 358.

10 The Dilemma of a South African Liberal: Nadine Gordimer's The Late Bourgeois World

▼▼▼▼▼▼▼▼▼▼▼▼▼▼▼▼▼▼▼▼▼▼▼▼▼▼▼▼▼▼

The Dilemma of White Liberals

The Late Bourgeois World[1] tells the story of the life and activities of Max and his former wife, Liz, the latter being the narrator. It relates their involvement in the politics of South Africa and Max's eventual death. Both are born into White families whose histories go back to the days of Cecil Rhodes and other magnates who made fortunes from gold mining in South Africa. Max's background is particularly envious as his father is an MP and the whole family enjoys a high reputation in the South African White society. So wealthy are the Van Den Sandts that it is not even necessary for Max to have professional training or to complete his studies at the university.

Despite his comfortable background, however, Max develops into an enlightened liberal. His liberalism, so disturbing and disconcerting to the old conservative members of the bourgeois class, reveals itself quite clearly on his sister's wedding day. When called upon to deliver a speech, Max advises the bride, Queenie, and the bridegroom, Allan, to be aware of 'a whole world' outside that of bourgeois society. He warns them against what he calls 'moral sclerosis'. With amazing eloquence and wit he describes the hard-heartedness and narrow-mindedness of White bourgeois society: 'The thing that makes them distribute free blankets in the location in winter, while refusing to pay wages people could live on' (p. 49).

So Max sees himself as someone with a commitment to the creation of a better society in South Africa. He gets involved in liberal-led multiracial gatherings and gets so trusted by some vociferous black politicians like Spears Qwabe that he becomes their guru (p. 78). In this, Max behaves like a typical liberal in a colonial situation, for it is characteristic of White liberals to pose as the champions of Black freedom and become the rallying point of certain groups of the Black intelligentsia. Sometimes this is done with ulterior motives – to pose as radicals and liberators of the Black man and at the same time to act as a powerful moderating influence on Black politics. Max, ultimately, is something of this kind of liberal who politicizes the Africans but does not want them to become radical Marxists: 'Although Max had been a member of a Communist cell at the

University, he did not take a strictly Marxist line in his attempts to give Africans some background for the evolution of their own political thinking' (p. 68). Hence, rather than participate in the activities of well-established and militant movements like the ANC of South Africa, Max prefers to pose as adviser and helper to Spears Qwabe whose brand of African socialism is clearly harmless, because it leans neither to the East nor to the West (p. 76).

But in spite of his zeal and spirit of commitment, Max is not a principled and level-headed liberal. He has no clear ideological line, for he shifts from one political persuasion to another. He starts off as a member of a communist cell at the university, then he joins the non-racial Liberal Party, afterwards he becomes a member of the Congress of Democrats before he sees his role as that of a guru among the likes of Spears Qwabe. It is not surprising that he ends up as a state witness, betraying those he had previously worked with. Liz, however, admires Max, and her admiration for him leads her into creating all sorts of excuses for his failure in life.

> He might have been a politician, even (it was in the family after all), if political ambitions outside the maintenance of white power had been recognized. He might have been a good revolutionary, if there had been a little more time, before all radical movements were banned, for him to acquire political discipline. *There are possibilities for me but under what stone do they lie?* (p. 74).

The last sentence is a quotation from Kafka which underlines Liz's interpretation of Max's failures: he would have succeeded had he been given a chance. But how can a revolution be condoned by oppressive authorities? How can a revolutionary wish the authorities to bless his radicalism? One becomes a revolutionary not because radical movements are given the licence to operate, but precisely because they are persecuted. Max's failure cannot be explained in terms of the oppressive system obtaining in South Africa. And his death is not a martyr's death. Max is the victim of his own immaturity. He is presented as someone who never completes anything. He leaves his studies unfinished, he shifts from one political party to another, he even abandons the cause for justice altogether and becomes a state witness – a complete reversal of everything he has been fighting for. It is therefore logical that he cannot live a full life – he drives himself into the sea and dies a frustrated failure.

Liz has the greatest admiration for Max, because although he failed he tried to do something. However, she herself is eventually an ineffective participant in the struggle for justice. Like Max, she is a liberal and, like him, she has broken through the cocoon of the colour bar and takes a human being as a human being. But unlike Max she is not a zealous theorizer and is rather more interested in doing practical things for the struggle. In the end she finds herself on the horns of a frightening dilemma: to be or not to be. Luke, a member of the banned Pan-African Congress movement, asks her to help his organization bring in money from overseas. In theory she can help by using her grandmother's account, but her final thoughts on the matter are an expression of fear:

I've been lying awake a long time, now. There is no clock in the room since the red travelling clock that Bobo gave me went out of order, but the slow, even beats of my heart repeat to me, like a clock; afraid, alive, afraid, alive, afraid, alive. (p. 160)

To be involved to the extent of meeting Luke's request is evidently to go too far for her. And if Liz succumbs to her fear, she fulfils Maxim Gorky's saying quoted at the beginning of the book: 'The madness of the brave is the wisdom of life.' To stay alive in South Africa one has to refrain from dangerous commitment. Those who try to go too far in their commitment will end up being buried in the sea – like Max.

Gordimer and Bourgeois Society

Nadine Gordimer's book goes beyond the mere depiction of the political activities of White liberals in South Africa. It is of much greater significance because it portrays the impending disintegration of White bourgeois society in the Republic. This society is characterized by serious internal contradictions. It is a society that is split in half: on the one hand is the old conservative bourgeoisie represented by the older members of the Van Den Sandts family. This section of White society is characterized by traditional bourgeois ethics: honour and respectability in public, going to church, advocating constitutional action as a means of social change, hypocrisy and so on. And in typical fashion, when Max is arrested on a charge of sabotage, his father, Theo Van Den Sandts, resigns his seat in Parliament: it is a disgrace to his family for his son to be involved in violent acts of sabotage against the state. The conservative bourgeoisie is intent on maintaining the status quo and keeping all power and wealth in the hands of the Whites. Its advocacy of constitutional reform is in effect meant to protect White interests, for it reserves for itself the sole right to introduce such changes.

On the other hand there is an emerging sub-class of young liberals, some of whom are, like Liz and her son Bobo, of a lower social status than the wealthy conservatives. This group is marked not only by its liberalism, but also by its unconventional social habits and its new code of morality. To this group, conventional Christian ethics are outmoded, marriage is not sacrosanct, divorce is 'one of those things', sex can be enjoyed with anybody – so long as there is mutual agreement – and babies, like Bobo, can be conceived in the back of a car! What is more, this section of White society is prepared to give Blacks some share of the country's wealth, and so people like Max can risk imprisonment in the name of what they consider to be social justice.

These two sections of the White bourgeois class are consequently at war with each other. This is seen in the behaviour of Max, who is clearly a rebel and a disgrace as far as the likes of Theo Van Den Sandts are concerned. He is depicted as being in conflict with his conservative father, and on Queenie's wedding day he takes the opportunity of presenting a direct affront to the assumptions of White society by warning Queenie and Allan against 'moral sclerosis'. But his words fall on deaf ears, for instead of contemplating on Max's speech which is evidently a radical departure from the conventional speeches given on such occasions, the audience is concerned about the customary toast. As Liz reports, 'In a little while nobody seemed to remember that the speech had been any different from dozens of others they'd sat through and didn't remember' (p. 50). The conservatives are determined to maintain the status quo and are so hardened in their ways that Max might as well have been talking to the wall. This conflict between conservatives and liberals marks a crisis in bourgeois ideology: the winds of change are beginning to blow across the White-dominated republic.

With this observation we come to the heart of the book and the significance of the title. Liz and Graham are talking about Max's death and a newspaper report on some American astronauts who have gone into space. Liz asks Graham what he thinks their age will be called, and it so happens that Graham has just read a book which describes the age as 'the Late Bourgeois World'. He goes on to explain the writer's ideological line: 'Yes, but the writer – he's an East German – uses it as a wider one – it covers the arts, religious beliefs, technology, scientific discoveries, love-making, everything' (p. 114). Graham goes on to explain that the East German communist writer would see the age in relation to what the former calls 'the early Communist World'. The seeds of the new world are already present in the existing social order.

But does this mean that a new social order is about to be born in South Africa? This is where Gordimer presents us with blurred visions. Although bourgeois society in the White-ruled republic is depicted as moribund, the author does not show us clearly what forces are to supersede it and bring about social change. We are shown representatives of various social classes such as the conservative bourgeoisie (e.g. Theo Van Den Sandts), the liberal bourgeoisie (Max, Liz, Graham), a weak example of the Black intelligentsia (Spears Qwabe), a spokesman for the nationalist movements (Luke Fokase), but there is no representative of the proletariat or the peasantry. So what force is to bring about change? The nationalist movement, perhaps? But the nationalist movement is hardly presented as a powerful agent of change.

The major force contributing to the disintegration of White bourgeois society is the rising liberal bourgeoisie, whose life-styles and attitude to race mark a frightening departure from the norms of conservatives. But this sub-class is not depicted as having history on its side either, for its champions end in the sea like Max, and in the bid to keep alive they fail to take sides with the forces of change, as in the case of Liz. Thus in the final analysis Gordimer fails to show who will be the agent of change, and how.

But this lack of commitment to any particular political group is deliberate, for it is in line with her own philosophy as a writer. Although she fights apartheid, Nadine Gordimer does not take a partisan line and is in this regard opposed to the Marxist viewpoint. She has declared,

Unlike Sartre, I believe a 'writer's morality' is valid, and the temptation to put one's writing at the service of a cause – whether it is fighting the colour-bar or 'the momentary renunciation of literature in order to educate people', etc., . . . is a betrayal.

She goes on to explain that she is 'not a politically-minded person by nature' and that she has 'come to the abstractions of politics through the flesh and blood of individual behaviour'.[2] Thus, socio-political problems are presented in terms of their effect on individual character and of the individual's response to them, not from a specific ideological standpoint.

There is consequently no millenium in Gordimer's vision. *The Late Bourgeois World* is not superseded by a socialist or communist world. The difference between the present and the future is symbolized by the antithesis between Max drowning in the sea and the American astronauts walking about in space: 'When Max drowned today, a man walked about in space' (p. 154). Even the mass media reflect this triumph of science over the present. Max is quickly dropped from the headlines as the focus is now on the space flight: 'Max was dropped from the late final edition, crowded out by astronauts' (pp. 152–3). Here is the triumph of science over current modes of thinking, but in Liz's mind the triumph of science does not mean a purely secular vision. The scientific search becomes identical with a spiritual search, for it is a yearning for eternity. The man of the future, unlike men of past epochs, will reach God through his scientific explorations rather than through religious worship:

What's going on overhead is perhaps the spiritual expression of our age, and we don't recognise it. Space exploration isn't a 'programme' . . . it's the new religion. Out of the capsule, up there, out of this world in a way you can never be, gone down to the sea bed; out of this world into infinity, eternity. Could any act of worship as we've known such things for two thousand years express more urgently a yearning for the life beyond life – the yearning for God? (p. 156).

Thus Gordimer merges the socio-political problem of South Africa with that of the future of mankind which she rather romanticizes. She succeeds in portraying her own vision as a Westerner, but leaves the reader with no real clue as to how the immediate problem in contemporary South Africa might be resolved or what specific direction the country is taking or might take. By speculating about the future of the post-bourgeois world and failing to depict the totality of the South African social scene and its conflicts more concretely, she falls short of capturing the mood of the epoch. *The Late Bourgeois World* is the work of a social democrat and may be cited as an example of critical realism. Of this novel we can say with Engels that realism does not only mean truth of detail, but also 'the truth in reproduction of typical characters under typical conditions'.[3] Gordimer's characters are typical enough, 'but the circumstances which surround them and make them act are not perhaps equally so'.[4] We are shown the activities of white liberals and their African associates – whose social background is not clear – but the agitation of the black South African masses which led to incidents like the massacres of Sharpeville and to the banning of political parties is not portrayed.

Language and Narrative Structure

In *The Late Bourgeois World*, as in *A World of Strangers*, Gordimer employs the first-person narrative technique, the 'I'. The story is not told from the point of view of the author, but from that of one of the major characters, Liz. The opening words and closing words of the book are hers.

The narrative starts at a very significant turning-point in Liz's life – the death of Max. Liz receives a telegram from Capetown telling her simply: *Max found drowned in car Capetown harbour*. Gordimer chooses her point of departure very well, for in a moment like this the bereaved is often overcome by a contemplative mood, with a feeling of affection for the dead. Suddenly Max occupies a very important place in Liz's consciousness and in her conception of life and the world. She relives in her imagination all she has gone through with Max – the child he gave her, the wedding, political activities and so on, in spite of the fact that she and Max had lived apart as divorcees. Her recollection of these things leads to a new understanding of Max and of life.

In order to explore Liz's life with Max, Graham and others effectively, the author employs the flashback technique. Thus in the first 'chapter' – for there are no real chapter divisions – the story takes place in the present, Liz's first reaction is to go and inform Bobo, her son by Max, that his father is dead. In the second 'chapter' we are taken back to Liz's past life: her marriage into the Van Den Sandt family, her early life and family background, Max's involvement in the Defiance Campaign of 1952, Max's participation in a 'terrorist' act, Queenie's wedding, etc. In the third 'chapter' we are brought back to the present. Liz is entering her flat after visiting Bobo and doing some shopping. By the time we come to page 93, just over halfway through the book, we have gained an insight into Max's life, but at every stage of the narrative we get echoes of the Max now buried under the waters of the sea. His life and his death are presented to us simultaneously.

It is important to note that the narrative takes place during the course of one day, a Saturday. Liz receives the telegram from Cape Town, goes to see Bobo, does her shopping, goes to see her grandmother at the Home, comes back to her flat and meets Graham again, takes Graham home, gets a visit from Luke Fokase, goes to sleep and sums up her fear of being involved in politics when she wakes up at night. That the narrative covers the duration of a day and a night is by no means fortuitous. In fact, it is a feat of ingenuity on the part of the author, for if the narrative had taken much longer, the significance of Max in Liz's consciousness would be lost; the sorrow and mood of contemplation resulting from bereavement is normally overcome after a short period of time. This is particularly true of cases like that of Liz, where the deceased is merely a former partner, a divorcee. Thus even in the narrative structure, Nadine Gordimer seeks to relate art to reality.

With regard to the linguistic format, there are a number of significant features. The style itself is abstract. For the most part, the tale is told in smooth, faultless language which at times moves like swift ripples of water, lending the narrative a lyric touch. What strikes the reader in the first pages is the taut and undecorative language, almost in the manner of Hemingway's style in *The Old Man and the Sea*. This abstractness of language can be taxing – though not to the same extent as Soyinka's – and where the author attempts to describe a scene, there is no clear picture presented to the reader's mind. Here is an example:

> The road to the school leads away from the hilly ridges of Johannesburg and soon strikes out straight through the mealie fields and flat high veld of the plain. It's early winter, it was one of those absolutely wind-still mornings filled with calm steady sunlight that make the few trees look black against the pale grass. All that was left of the frost overnight was the fresh smell. There was an old pepper tree here and there, where there must once have been a farmhouse; eucalyptus with tattered curls of bark, twiggy acacias, mud-walls of an abandoned hut; an Indian store; a yellowing willow beside a crack in the earth. (p. 11)

The tendency to abstract is often a reflection of Liz's intellectual mind. She is given to theorizing, to comprehending reality through intellectual reflection, as in the following passage:

> There was one of those sunsets beginning – the kind we've been having for months . . . People carry their drinks outside not so much to look at the light, as to be in it. It's everywhere, surrounding faces and air as it does the trees. It comes from a volcanic eruption on the other side of the world, from particles of dust that have risen to the upper atmosphere. Some people think it's from the atomic tests; but it's said that, in Africa, we are safe from atomic fall-out from the Northern Hemisphere because of the doldrums, an area where the elements lie becalmed and carry no pollution. (p. 106)

The abstract style is combined with an absence of emotional appeal. The narrative is dry, intellectual, so sifted of emotional overtones that even the description of the sex act becomes something of a scientific analysis. In this passage Liz is describing her sexual experiences with Graham:

> Yet when he's inside me – last night – there's the strangest thing. He's much better than someone my own age, he comes to me with a solid and majestic erection that will last as long as we choose. Sometimes he will be in me for an hour and I can put my hand on my belly and feel the blunt head, like a standard upheld, through my flesh. But while he fills me, while you'd think

the last gap in me is closed forever, while we lie there silent I get the impression that I am the one who has drawn him up into my flesh, I am the one who holds him there, that I am the one who has him, helpless. (p. 61)

But Liz can be down to earth in her speech as in the following passage where she sums up her non-ethnocentric attitudes in terms that are a combination of scientific (medical) language and frank down to earth language. The use of words like 'shit' and 'urine' not only marks the liberal bourgeoisie's departure from the canons of linguistic behaviour observed by the conservative bourgeoisie, but is also an expression of the ability of the former to see the absurdity of the practice of separating people on the grounds of race and colour:

> I've got my job analysing stools for tapeworm and urine for bilharzia and blood for cholesterol (at the Institute for Medical Research). And so we keep our hands clean. So far as work is concerned, at least. Neither of us makes money out of cheap labour or performs a service confined to people of a particular colour. For myself, thank God shit and blood are all the same, no matter whom they come from. (p. 60)

And though her language tends to be all bony without flesh and blood, in the manner of T. S. Eliot's poetry, Nadine Gordimer can occasionally inject intense feeling into her narrative, can evoke disgust or resentment for the object of description. The best example of this is the merciless and witty irony with which Liz describes the state of old women who are decaying with age at the Home where her grandmother has been relegated:

> Among the very small white-haired old ladies, the dying diabetic, taking so long to die, was still there, humped on her side, smoking. She has the reckless drinker's face that diabetics sometimes have, and looks as if she had once been good-looking like a finished whore. But the distinguishing marks of social caste are often distorted by illness; the home is not cheap and it is unlikely that she belongs to anything other than the respectable middle class. The monster with the enormous belly was sitting on a chair with her legs splayed out, like a dead frog swollen on a pond. I have never known what is the matter with her. (p. 96)

To appreciate Gordimer's technique the reader should take stock of the fact that Liz is a liberal whose opposition to the standard assumptions of White bourgeois society drives her to expose the ugly side of that society. On one level the description can be taken to symbolize the disintegration of self-centred and hypocritical traditional values. On another level Liz's reaction to the state of these dying middle-class women is meant to expose the true humanity that the class shares with all human beings, White or Black. When they were young, lively and beautiful, these old ladies were part of a society that discriminated against the Blacks, who are considered filthy and sub-human. Where is White superiority now when a granddaughter's reaction to her grandmother is one of mingled affection and revulsion?

There is little to say about the revelation of character through language in this book. The novel is written in conventional mother-tongue English. The characters whose idiolect is marked by any quality of distinctiveness are the Afrikaaner nurse at the old people's home, whose idiom is certainly not that of a mother-tongue speaker, and Spears Qwabe, whose idiolect is marked by such colloquial words as 'chaps', 'man', 'commies' and by some deviant structures. Of Spears Qwabe's English Liz says: 'It was the beat in his voice spacing the political clichés, grammatical constructions translated from Xhosa and literal translations from Afrikaans, of his strong-flavoured English.' (p. 79) The other African, Luke Fokase, also has something of Spears's idiolect, but his is not highly marked. The book is clearly dominated by Liz's idiolect, which evidently reflects the author's own language. Indeed, the use of the first person point of view has the disadvantage of reducing stylistic variation in the depiction of character. Even where other characters are supposed to be speaking we are aware all the time that the narrator is reporting. Can the narrator report accurately the conversations of other people?

Another disadvantage of this technique is that readability is adversely affected. We know the story teller is alive and well, for she is telling the story: no harm can come to her. Readability is further affected by the author killing off one of the two main characters on the first page. If one main character is dead and the other is relating the story, what is there to expect or to fear? There is no suspense. The prose is quite good, but there is no fascination or compelling power to the book.

Be that as it may, Nadine Gordimer has told a profound story. The content element is unbalanced – in that we are not given a complete picture of the South African socio-political situation – but the different parts of the book hang together as one piece, and the characters, though mostly flat, are plausible. This is one of those books written by a White South African which deserve the attention of African scholars.

Notes

1 *The Late Bourgeois World*, London, Jonathan Cape, 1966.
2 Quoted from J. Vinson, *Contemporary Novelists*, p. 501.
3 Engels to Margaret Harkness, *On Literature and Art*, p.90.
4 Ibid., p. 90. See also Craig (ed.) *Marxists on Literature*, pp. 269–70.

11   Ideology, Form and Social Vision in the African Novel: Overview and Conclusions

▼▼▼▼▼▼▼▼▼▼▼▼▼▼▼▼▼▼▼▼▼▼▼▼▼▼▼▼▼▼▼▼▼

Authorial and Aesthetic Ideology

In this closing chapter we shall attempt to give a general view of the relationship between art and ideology in African literature by exploring aspects of ideology which are not discussed in the preceding chapters. Our focus is on three categories of ideology: the dominant ideology or ideologies, authorial ideology and aesthetic ideology.

By the dominant ideology of an epoch we mean the beliefs, assumptions and set of values that inform the thoughts and actions of a people in a particular historical moment. Ideology here refers to what Goran Therborn calls 'that aspect of the human condition under which human beings live their lives as conscious actors in a world that makes sense to them to varying degrees'. Ideology is 'the medium through which this consciousness and meaningfulness operates.'[1]

In a situation where there are competing ideologies, a writer will project his own ideological stance which may or may not be homologous with the dominant ideology. Whatever ideological stance he adopts will be referred to here as his authorial ideology. It is therefore reasonable to assume that in a continent as large as Africa we should expect to find a whole range of ideologies operating in the literary sphere. These ideologies may be defined in political terms as conservatism, liberalism, humanism, nationalism, radicalism or revolutionary democracy, Marxism and so on. It is important to concede that works of art are not political statements, but the fact is that there is no facet of life which operates outside the sphere of ideology.

Aesthetic ideology refers to the literary convention and stylistic stances adopted by the writer. Eagleton sees aesthetic ideology as a complex formation constituted by a number of levels, namely, 'theories of literature, critical practices, literary traditions, *genres*, conventions, devices and discourses.'[2] Literary movements – romanticism, symbolism, expressionism, realism, formalism etc. – are all characterized by identifiable assumptions about the nature of literature and the forms and styles that are appropriate to it. When Engels defined realism as a literary ideology he did not define it solely in terms of social vision. He commended Margaret Harkness for the style she adopted in writing her novel *City Girl*. Consequently realism is not just a matter of telling the story truthfully and depicting typical characters under typical circumstances; it also involves avoiding complicated stylization and artificial adornments.[3]

Realism thus involves the adoption of authorial ideology *and* an aesthetic ideology. The aesthetic ideology of realism as defined by Engels was carried over into socialist art so that while a critical realist and a socialist realist comprehend reality differently, they share the same views in respect of how the writer should represent reality. The simplicity of a realist artist does not only operate on the level of style or the linguistic format, it is also discernible in the narrative structure. The plots of realist and socialist novels which are modelled on the classical conception of realism are linear and chronological. This is true of nineteenth century realist novels such as those of Tolstoy and also of socialist novels like Gorky's *Mother* and Sholokhov's *And Quiet Flows the Don*.

It would be wrong to ascribe realism to socialist artists only for it became the dominant movement in western Europe from the nineteenth century until it was challenged by other literary movements in the twentieth century. One of the most important of these movements is *modernism*, the aesthetic ideology that is characteristic of the novels of Virginia Woolf, James Joyce and D. H. Lawrence. Whereas realist writers are concerned with depicting social reality and the social factors which influence man's life, modernist fiction is concerned with exploring states of mind, man's consciousness and the sub-conscious. One of the most illuminating formulations of modernism has been given by David Lodge in *The Modes of Modern Writing*. From that formulation we can extract the following characteristics:

1. Modernist fiction is concerned with the inner man and explores the workings of the mind through a process of introspection.
2. As the writer focuses on this internal 'reality' external reality and social issues are given minimum attention or are almost completely ignored.
3. The importance of plot is greatly reduced in the writer's ordering of events and he conveys his meaning largely through a complicated system of para-linguistic affective devices such as allusion, images and symbolism – hence modernist fiction tends to be highly metaphorical.
4. The linear plot is dispensed with and time is collapsed in the present or the novel moves backwards and forth in time perspective.[4]

The important thing for our purposes is that in our analysis of African literature we should be aware of these and other aesthetic ideologies, though our point of reference will be realism in its two forms – critical and socialist. Many African novelists – Achebe, the early Ngugi, Ekwensi, Aluko, Mungoshi and others – tend to write in the classical realist fashion. This may be explained by saying that the early African novel was shaped by two major influences. First, most of the fiction the writer was exposed to was written in the critical realist mode. Secondly, the linear structure of classical realism is similar to the structure of African folk tales which follow a chronological form of presentation.

Liberalism and Realism – Nadine Gordimer

Nadine Gordimer is cited in this book as an example of liberal democracy, but she has developed in social outlook over the years and may now consider herself a socialist.[5] Whatever the case, the comment here is based on *The Late Bourgeois World* which in ideological terms may be put in the same category as Alan Paton's *Cry, the Beloved Country* and Doris Lessing's *The Grass Is Singing*. But in terms of the author's analysis of racial problems in Southern Africa, Gordimer is more successful than her fellow white writers. Although she is not completely successful in portraying the South African social scene in its totality, Gordimer's vision is more complete and more real than that of either Paton or Lessing. Her characters – Elizabeth, Max, Graham, Luke Fokase and Theo Van Den Sandt – are sufficiently convincing as representatives of their respective social groups. Her liberals are not idealized like those of Paton, and although her Africans are not given sufficient prominence, they possess their own consciousness and are not presented to us through the eyes of white people like Doris Lessing's 'natives' in *The Grass Is Singing*.

The Late Bourgeois World is modernist in form. There is no omniscient intrusive narrator. The novel is told in the first person with Elizabeth as the narrator whose consciousness the author explores using the internal monologue. There is no linear plot in the novel. The events take place in one day, but through a series of flashbacks we see the past and present of Liz's life and that of the other characters until we emerge with a clear picture of what has gone on and how the heroine finds herself where she is. Gordimer's use of the interior monologue is interesting in that Elizabeth never loses touch with the external world. In fact internal reflection and external reality are neatly interlocked for Elizabeth is a character who is aware of the reality around her. She is involved in social activities, and when she is engaged in introspection her mind takes her again and again to concrete events and issues, and this is how we see the reality of the South African situation unfolding before us. In her honest and truthful depiction of the activities, failures and dilemmas of white liberals, and in her unpatronizing treatment of African characters, Gordimer assumes an ideological posture which is more progressive than that of liberal democracy.

Nationalism and Critical Realism – Chinua Achebe

If Paton, Lessing and Gordimer are taken as projecting various shades of liberalism and liberal democracy a significant number of the pre-independence phase writers can be said to be 'nationalist' in ideological orientation. As explained in Chapter Four writers like Chinua Achebe, Camara Laye, Peter

Abrahams, the early Ngugi and others were part and parcel of the African nationalist movement, and felt the same compulsion as political ideologists to reclaim and assert the freedom, independence and values of the African people. Some of the works produced by these authors are overtly political. Examples are Peter Abrahams' *A Wreath for Udomo*, Tim Aluko's *One Man One Matchet* and William Conton's *The African*. Others display a concern with cultural nationalism as opposed to political nationalism. Chief among these are Achebe's *Things Fall Apart* and *Arrow of God*, Camara Laye's *The African Child* and Ngugi's *The River Between*. Most of the works cited here are, in terms of aesthetic ideology, written in the critical realist mode. In some cases realism is coloured by idealism when the African past is sentimentalized and romanticized. Camara Laye's *The African Child* typifies this victory of nationalistic idealism over realism. Laye writes in the négritude tradition whose portrayal of the beauty and positive qualities of the African past is often subjective and falsified. The African past – compared to the present-day Africa contaminated by Western influences – assumes the shape of a utopia, a rather naively idealized world free from defects, conflicts and moral degeneracy.

Things Fall Apart and *Arrow of God* are just as infused with the spirit of cultural nationalism as *The African Child*. Achebe's position on the responsibility of the writer in educating his people to appreciate their own culture is made abundantly clear in the essay in which he declares that as a writer he is concerned with 'the fundamental theme' which must first be disposed of. 'This theme – put quite simply – is that African people did not hear of culture for the first time from Europeans; that their societies were not mindless but frequently had a philosophy of great depth and value and beauty, that they had poetry and, above all, they had dignity.'[6]

For the writer to be able to perform this function well, Achebe goes on to say, he must have 'a proper sense of history'. In Achebe's scheme of things having a proper sense of history means not only being able to explain what it is that African societies have lost as a result of the encroachment of colonialism but also presenting a true and realistic picture of the African past. Thus in both *Things Fall Apart* and *Arrow of God* we are given the picture of an Igbo society that was highly organized and deeply religious, a society which valued bravery, hard work, material wealth as well as eloquence and dignity – a society that possessed an enviable culture. At the same time, Achebe does not hesitate to expose the weaknesses and less attractive aspects of this culture. There is, for instance, the cruelty exemplified by Okonkwo's axing of Ikemefuna; people who commit certain crimes – even accidental killing – are exiled from their homes, like Okonkwo who is banished for seven years; the whole society is riddled with superstitious beliefs and fears.

In depicting the disintegration of Igbo culture in both *Things Fall Apart* and *Arrow of God* Achebe does not give us a partial or biased view of the historical epoch he is dealing with. He makes use of a wide variety of characters to represent different points of view and social groups. In *Arrow of God*, for instance, Ezeulu, Nwaka and Akuebue represent the chief priest and elders of traditional society; Captain Winterbottom and Clarke are representatives of colonial administrators with different personalities, while Brown, Goodcountry and Onachukwu stand for various approaches to the evangelization of Africans. Thus we are able to see how political, religious, tribal and personal factors all contributed to the crumbling of the traditional social structure. Although the encroachment of the white man's civilization and political power features as the principal catalyst in this change, Achebe does not exonerate his ancestors from blame. Ezeulu's pride and unbending character and his personal conflicts with Nwaka are partly responsible for what happens. The author consequently succeeds in presenting a truthful and balanced account of reality and is able to capture the mood of the epoch. His method is that of objective realism.

Achebe typifies what has become the commonest version of African realism. His linear plots are not only an imitation of the African traditional story, but also coincide with the structure of nineteenth-century European realist fiction. And, just as the nineteenth-century European realists presented a critique of capitalism in non-Marxist terms, Achebe attacks cultural imperialism and post-independence corruption in what may be termed 'moderate' terms. He certainly presents a progressive view of history. He aligns himself with anti-colonialist forces in *Arrow of God* and *Things Fall Apart* and is critical of the rampant corruption and misdemeanours of the emerging African ruling class in *No Longer At Ease* and *A Man of the People*, but he only goes so far and no further. He does not present a Marxist or in any way radical view of social problems, but he succeeds in giving us a truthful account of what he portrays. His characters are typical and the circumstances under which they operate are natural and convincing. In the two 'old world' novels where he gives a truthful account of Igbo society without glossing over its weaknesses and despite his declared intention to dispose of 'the fundamental theme', his art becomes a model of the triumph of realism over the claims of nationalism.

Radicalism, Metaphoric and Mythic Realism – Ayi Kwei Armah

Armah's stance against corruption, neo-colonialism and imperialism is not couched in terms that can in any sense be called moderate. It is decidedly militant or radical in the sense that it is expressed in vigorous, harsh, passionate and uncompromising terms. Armah is a revolutionary but he is not a Marxist writer. No informed reader can deny that *Two Thousand Seasons* is influenced by Marxism, as was explained in Chapter Six. It can be argued, for instance, that his ideological stance is consonant with socialism in so far as he takes a clearly partisan line – he is decidedly on the side of the oppressed. It is also arguable that the view of African history presented in *Two Thousand Seasons* is consistent with historical materialism. According to the Marxist conception of history man has passed through various stages of social development from primitive communalism through slave societies, feudalism, capitalism and socialism to the highest and final stage which is yet to be achieved – communism. In Armah's book African history passes through similar phases. The first stage is marked by an idealized form of egalitarianism when the people followed the way – this is the phase which inspires the prophetess Anoa. She wants the African people to return to the values of that period. The next decisive stage follows the period of contact between Africans and the Arabs. It was this phase which marked the rise of zombis, askaris and other forces of oppression. It was also through the influence of the Arabs that kings like Koranche arose to oppress the people. The period of contact with Arabs is followed by the coming of the destroyers from the sea who bring with them capitalism, colonialism and the slave-trade. This phase is followed by the neo-colonial phase when leaders like Kamuzu have replaced colonial rulers. Then comes the stage of an armed liberation struggle which gives rise to hopes of a genuine return to the way. This final stage is the millenium which the African people should hope for and fight for. It is a stage which parallels Marx's vision of a classless society under communism.

As explained in Chapter Six, Armah's vision is couched in racial rather than class terms. All Europeans and Arabs are White destroyers. There is no distinction between revolutionary and oppressive classes among them.

Furthermore, the African millenium is not brought about by what would be called revolutionary classes in Marxism, it is not brought about by the proletariat or an alliance of workers, peasants and revolutionary intellectuals, but by a group of young militants who have been initiated into the traditions of the people of the way. In *The Healers* the forces of change are represented by a group of professionals, the healers, who, like the utterers in *Two Thousand Seasons*, are the embodiment of traditional values. Damfo, the leader of the healers, believes in an egalitarian society without slaves and kings, but that society is brought about through a process of spiritual and ideological education which does not involve the class struggle. Armah's vision is clearly characterized by a form of idealism which makes his conception of socialism utopian rather than scientific. But to say this is by no means to belittle his artistic achievement, but to clear certain misconceptions about his authorial ideology.

Armah's novels are revolutionary in both content and form. That he was a revolutionary writer became evident when he published his first novel, *The Beautyful Ones Are Not Yet Born*, a devastating critique of post-independence corruption and neo-colonialism in Nkrumah's Ghana. Corruption is portrayed in terms of a pattern of images and symbols which denote filth and dirt. Throughout the length of the book there is a constant reference to shit, urine, excreta, vomit and other forms of filth. The walls of a latrine are marked by 'large chunks of various shit', a bus driver spits 'a generous gob of mucus', Koomson's mouth had 'the rich stench of rotten menstrual blood' and his insides give 'an inner fart of personal, corrupt thunder', and so on.

These images are not only meant to elicit a certain response in the reader; they are richly symbolic. Filth is used everywhere as a symbol of the corruption and moral depravity of politicians. The ugliness of the language is a reflection of the ugliness of the corruption which the author sets out to expose. The overall effect is to portray a nation which is labouring under a corrosive sickness. In fact the theme of the book is conveyed in metaphorical terms. Characters are not just ordinary realistic characters. They are symbolic. The main character is nameless; he is simply 'the man', symbolizing the common man who is the victim of the corrosive sickness as well as the individual who tries to stand outside this despicable moral depravity. Similarly his friend is simply called 'Teacher'. There are characters with individual names such as Koomson, but they too assume a metaphoric shape. Koomson is a typical character, a typical example of a corrupt government official. But this is not simply conveyed in terms of his deeds and behaviour – it is expressed in terms of the filth that he emits. He is so corrupt that he pollutes other people – even the man is polluted by Koomson. Looked at this way the following sentences assume a much greater significance than their literal meaning suggests:

> The man held his breath until the new smell had gone in the mixture with the liquid atmosphere of the Party man's farts filling the room. At the same time Koomson's insides gave a growl longer than usual, an inner fart of personal, corrupt thunder which in its fullness sounded as if it had rolled down all the way from the eating throat thundering through the belly and the guts, to end in further silent pollution of the air already thick with flatulent fear. (pp. 191–2)

There is no need to cite more examples of Armah's use of metaphor in *The Beautyful Ones Are Not Yet Born* because what has been said so far is common knowledge. What we intend to discover is his aesthetic ideology. Does Armah use the realistic mode, in other words? Although he tells his story truthfully, and in fact bluntly, he does not comply with Engels' other criterion of telling the story plainly 'without artificial complications and adornments'. He conveys his meaning through a complex pattern of symbols. Armah is not only concerned with projecting a radical critique of society, but seeks to do so in a highly artistic and metaphorical form. To this extent Ayi Kwei Armah marks a radical departure from the classical realism typified by Achebe – he writes in a modernist fashion. We have already seen that the use of metaphor to convey meanings is one characteristic feature of modernism. What we need to add here is that modernist writers tend to place more emphasis on form than do classical realists. In this respect Armah's *The Beautyful Ones Are Not Yet Born* is closer to Gabriel Okara's richly metaphorical novel, *The Voice*, than it is to such novels as Ngugi's *A Grain of Wheat* and Achebe's *A Man of the People* which deal with the same theme of disillusionment with the ruling petty bourgeois class in Africa, but in a much more direct way.

Because Armah's art is so richly metaphorical, it is not enough to describe his novel as simply 'modernist', for not all modernist novels are so richly metaphorical, and in any case Armah does not show some of the characteristic features of modernism outlined above. For instance all his art is committed, it is about social man, and does not concern itself with states of mind at the expense of external reality. Its concerns are the same as those of classical realists and socialist novelists. To distinguish the fictional mode of the *The Beautyful Ones Are Not Yet Born* from that of novels written in the classical realist mode we shall use the term *metaphoric realism* to refer to the former. The distinction between the two modes is as follows: in metaphoric realism the artist does not convey his meanings in a direct prosaic manner and is not merely concerned with depicting natural or life-like characters as in classical realism. His characters and the conditions under which they operate are no less real than those of classical realism, but they are consciously conceived as artistic representations of reality. The artist is not satisfied with a mere naturalistic imitation of reality, but wishes to invest that reality with an artistic form. Because he conveys his meanings through images and other forms of indirect reference, his language is more poetic than the language of classical realism. Thus Okara's *The Voice* and Achebe's *A Man of the People* are both realistic novels but while the latter is a good example of classical realism or what in more precise terms should be called *natural realism*, Okara's novel conveys its meanings through a wide range of para-linguistic affective devices – symbolism, atmosphere, allusion, dramatization and other devices.

Two Thousand Seasons and *The Healers* are historical novels. However, the former is not strictly speaking an historical novel. It is highly metaphorical and has something in common with *The Beautyful Ones Are Not Yet Born*. As an historical novel it has certain features in common with *The Healers*, but while the latter novel is based on a concrete historical moment, a particular aspect of Asante history in the nineteenth century, *Two Thousand Seasons* takes as its subject the whole fantastic sweep of African history, spans a period of one thousand years and is based on a mythical reconstruction of Africa's past and future. However, it is neither pure myth nor mere fantasy. Like an epic, *Two Thousand Seasons* is an amalgam of myth, history and fiction. In terms of realism, therefore, it belongs to a class of its own and cannot be put in the same category as *The Beautyful Ones Are Not Yet Born*. An appropriate term for this mode is *mythic realism*, a term which signifies the two most important aspects of the novel – it is constructed upon a mythical past, but addresses itself to real historical, ideological and political issues. True, Armah has extended the novel from beyond the boundaries of normal fiction by making use of African myths and oral traditions, but his novel offers significant insights into the human world in general and the African predicament in particular and can legitimately claim a place among realistic works.

Armah's radical authorial ideology is matched by an equally revolutionary aesthetic ideology which manifests itself in various forms, including his handling of the English language. He is unusually blunt and even vulgar in his description of sex and other physical appetites, his tone is charged with intense feelings and, as noted in Chapter Five, he remoulds the English language so that it becomes a fit medium for promoting the African revolution. Indeed, Armah's revolution is an Africa-centred revolution. Starting with *Why Are We So Blest?* we see an increasing pre-occupation with African values until in the last two novels there is a definite appeal for a return to African traditions. Thus we can conclude that the author's deviation from orthodox Marxism is consistent with his declared social vision.

Socialist Art and the Socialist Vision – Ngugi, Ousmane and La Guma

God's Bits of Woods, Petals of Blood and *In the Fog of the Seasons' End* are taken here as examples of socialist art. Other novels which fit into the category are Sahle Sellassie's *Firebrands*,[7] Pepetela's *Mayombe*[8] and Ngugi wa Thiong'o's *Devil on the Cross*. In all these novels the conflict is portrayed in terms of class, from the point of view of workers, peasants and other patriotic forces. In each story characters represent different classes and class interests as well as conflicting ideological standpoints.

Sembène Ousmane and Ngugi are evidently aware not only of the necessity to present a Marxist interpretation of reality but of the need to meet the requirements of socialist art. The story of *God's Bits of Wood* is not only told simply and truthfully as in criticial realist and socialist art; it also has a linear plot, a feature it shares with the novels of Sholokhov and other writers of 'socialist realist' fiction. In *God's Bits of Wood* all events lead to the final meeting between the workers and the management in Dakar, a meeting which results in victory for the workers. The inexorable march of history is dramatically symbolized by the march of the women from Thiès to Dakar. Both Ousmane and Ngugi follow an accepted principle of socialist art – the assimilation of positive foreign and bourgeois elements into their revolutionary art. Ngugi fulfils another requirement of realist and socialist art – from a Marxist point of view. In *Petals of Blood* we see a conscious effort to go beyond a mere photographic representation of reality, beyond 'superficial naturalism'. As explained in Chapter Eight, Ngugi penetrates into the essence of reality and sees the connection between the individual and his environment. But in some ways Ngugi's method of presentation departs quite significantly from that of classical realism and the conventional socialist novel. His plot is not linear for instance. Events do move forward, but they are not presented in a purely chronological manner. The flashback technique is used quite extensively alongside other complicated devices. The book also abounds in symbolism and other forms of reference discussed in Chapter Eight. There is, therefore, a strong tendency towards modernism in Ngugi, a tendency that is already apparent in *A Grain of Wheat* where he exploits the flashback technique quite effectively and displays a capacity to probe the deepest thoughts of his characters.

In Marxist terms authorial ideology in La Guma, Ngugi and Ousmane is characterized by true consciousness because these authors are able to see clearly the antagonistic forces operating in a particular epoch and to present an accurate analysis of society.

They are able to distinguish clearly between the dominators and the oppressed and to see the direction in which society is likely to move. Consequently they are able to write 'from the standpoint of the class which has prepared the broadest solutions for the most pressing problems afflicting human society.' But authorial ideology should not be confused with artistic excellence. *In the Fog of the Seasons' End, Petals of Blood* and *God's Bit of Wood* happen to rank among the best works of art to have come out of Africa to date, but this is not to say that there are no non-socialist novels of equal value. Sellassie's *Firebrands* is a socialist novel, but it is certainly not of greater artistic value than Achebe's *A Man of the People*. Ngugi's second socialist novel, *Devil on the Cross*, seems to mark a decline in the author's artistic achievement and is an inferior work of art to *A Grain of Wheat* which is only a transitional novel in Ngugi's development from critical realism to socialist art. A work of art cannot be judged on the basis of ideological content alone. Ideological content must be seen in relation to aesthetic value. It is also arguable that some socialist writers tend to project a utopian view of society. This is true of those writers who accept literally Marx's vision of a Communist world free from all forms of oppression and exploitation. This utopian view of human history is discernible in the concluding paragraph of *Petals of Blood*:

> Tomorrow it would be the workers and the peasants leading the struggle and seizing power to overturn the system of all its preying bloodthirsty gods and gnomic angels, bringing to an end the reign of the few over the many and the era of drinking blood and feasting on human flesh. Then, only then, would the kingdom of man and woman really begin, they joying and loving in creative labour. (p. 344)

Implicit in these words is the suggestion that once capitalism has been defeated in Kenya an ideal society free of all forms of exploitation will emerge. The author's view is that socialism is an ideal to fight for since its aim is to end the exploitation of man by man, to reduce inequality and to improve the quality of life for everyone, but it is important to admit that contradictions can never be completely wiped out. There will always be a need to keep an eye on those individuals and groups who want to abuse their power and positions for their own self-aggrandizement. This is the reality that has been unfolding before our eyes since the advent of socialism, a reality which is truthfully depicted in the works of one of the greatest masters of realism, Mikhail Sholokhov.

Notes

1 Goran Therborn, *The Ideology of Power and the Power of Ideology*, p. 2.
2 T. Eagleton, *Criticism and Ideology*, p. 60.

3 See Marx and Engels, *On Literature and Art*, p. 90.

4 See D. Lodge, *The Modes of Modern Writing*, pp. 45–6.

5 She made a statement to this effect at the First Zimbabwe International Book Fair Writers' Workshop held in Harare in August 1983.

6 See Chinua Achebe, 'The Role of the Writer in a New Nation', in G. D. Killam (ed.), *African Writers on African Writing*, London, Heinemann, 1973, p. 8.

7 B. M. Sahle Sellassie, *Firebrands*, Harlow, Longman, Drumbeat, 1979.

8 Pepetela (Artur Carlos Mauricio Pestana dos Santos), *Mayombe*, Harare, Zimbabwe Publishing House, 1983 (translated from the 1980 Portuguese edition by Michael Wolfers), London, Heinemann, African Writers Series 269, 1984.

Bibliography

Achebe, C. (1958) *Things Fall Apart*, London, Heinemann African Writers Series 1 (1962).

Achebe, C. (1964) *Arrow of God*, London, Heinemann African Writers Series 16 (revised edition 1974).

Afanasyev, V. G. (1980) *Marxist Philosophy*, Moscow, Progress Publishers.

Althusser, L. (1971) *Lenin and Philosophy and Other Essays*, London, New Left Books.

Armah, A. K. (1974) *Why Are We So Blest?* London, Heinemann African Writers Series 155.

Armah, A. K. (1978 *The Healers*, Nairobi, East African Publishing House and London, Heinemann African Writers Series 194.

Armah, A. K. (1979) *Two Thousand Seasons*, Nairobi, East African Publishing House and London, Heinemann African Writers Series 218.

Arvon, H. (1977) *Marxist Esthetics*, Ithaca, New York, Cornell University Press.

Basin, Y. (1979) *Semantic Philosophy of Art*, Moscow, Progress Publishers.

Belyaev, A. (1978) *The Ideological Struggle and Literature*, Moscow, Progress Publishers.

Cabral, A. (1973) *Return to Source: Selected Speeches of Amilcar Cabral* (ed. Africa Information Service), New York, Monthly Review Press.

Caudwell, C. (1971) *Studies and Further Studies in a Dying Culture*, New York and London, Monthly Review Press, Modern Reader Edition (1972).

Conton, W. (1960) *The African*, London, Heinemann African Writers Series 12 (1964).

Craig, D. (1975) (ed.) *Marxists on Literature: An Anthology*, Harmondsworth, Penguin.

Dathorne, O. R. (1975) *African Literature in the Twentieth Century*, London, Heinemann.

Diop, Cheikh Anta (1974) *The African Origin of Civilization: Myth or Reality*, Westport, Lawrence Hill and Company.

Eagleton, T. (1976) *Marxism and Literary Criticism*, London, Methuen & Company.

Eagleton, T. (1978) *Criticism and Ideology*, London, Verso.

Eliot, T. S. (1963) *Collected Poems 1909-1962*, London, Faber & Faber.

Fanon, F. (1980) *The Wretched of the Earth*, Harmondsworth, Penguin.

Fischer, E. (1963) *The Necessity of Art: A Marxist Approach*, Harmondsworth, Penguin.

Fischer, E. (1970) *Marx in His Own Words*, Harmondsworth, Penguin.

Fraser, R. (1980) *The Novels of Ayi Kwei Armah*, London, Heinemann.

Fromm, E. (1961) *Marx's Concept of Man*, New York, Frederick Ungar Publishing Company.

Gordimer, N. (1966) *The Late Bourgeois World*, London, Jonathan Cape and Harmondsworth, Penguin.

Gorky, M. *On Literature*, Moscow, Progress Publishers.

Hyman, R. (1972) *Strikes*, London, Fontana.

Kadhani, M. and Zimunya, M. (1981) *And Now the Poets Speak*, Gweru, Mambo Press.

Khrapchenko, M. (1979) 'Literature and Art in Today's World', *Social Sciences*, Vol. X, No. 3, 83–102.

La Guma, A. (1972) *In the Fog of the Seasons' End*, London, Heinemann African Writers Series 110.

Laye, C. (1959) *The African Child*, London, Fontana.

Lenin, V. I. (1972) *Collected Works*, Vol. 10, Moscow, Progress Publishers.

Lenin, V. I. (1974) *Collected Works*, Vol. 16, Moscow, Progress Publishers.

Lenin, V. I. (1975a) *On Literature and Art*, Moscow, Progress Publishers.

Lenin, V. I. (1975b) 'Articles on Tolstoy', in Craig, D., *Marxists on Literature*, Harmondsworth, Penguin.

Lenin, V. I. (1975c) *On Socialist Ideology*, Moscow, Progress Publishers.

Lessing, D. (1973) *The Grass Is Singing*, London, Heinemann African Writers Series 131.

Lodge, D. (1977) *The Modes of Modern Writing*, London, Edward Arnold, paperback edition, 1979.

Ludowyk, E. F. C. (1979) *Understanding Shakespeare*, New Delhi, Vikas Publishing House.

Lukács, G. (1978a) *Studies in European Realism*, London, The Merlin Press.

Lukács, G. (1978b) *Writer and Critic*, London, The Merlin Press.

Lukács, G. (1981) *The Historical Novel*, Harmondsworth, Penguin.

Maillu, D. G. (1973) *My Dear Bottle*, Nairobi, Comb Books.

Maillu, D. G. (1974) *After 4.30*, Nairobi, Comb Books.

Mao Tse-Tung, (1975) 'Talks at the Yenan Forum on Literature and Art, *Selected Works of Mao Tse-Tung*, Vol. III, Peking, Foreign Language Press.

Marcuse, H. (1979) *The Aesthetic Dimension: Toward a Critique of Marxist Aesthetics*, London, Macmillan (Papermac).

Marx, K. and Engels, F. (1975) *Manifesto of the Communist Party*, Moscow, Progress Publishers.

Marx, K. and Engels, F. (1976) *On Literature and Art*, Moscow, Progress Publishers.

Ngara, E. A. (1974) 'The Significance of Time and Motion in the Poetry of T. S. Eliot: With Special Reference to the Teaching of Eliot in Rhodesia', University of London, M. Phil. thesis.

Ngara, E. A. (1980) 'Art and Ideology in the Novels of Ngugi wa Thiong'o', Seminar on Literature and Language 1980-1 Series, National University of Lesotho, Paper No. 2.

Ngara, E. A. (1982) *Stylistic Criticism and the African Novel*, London, Heinemann.

Ngugi, wa Thiong'o (1964) *Weep Not Child*, London, Heinemann African Writers Series 7.

Ngugi, wa Thiong'o (1965) *The River Between*, London, Heinemann African Writers Series 17.

Ngugi, wa Thiong'o (1967) *A Grain of Wheat*, London, Heinemann African Writers Series 36.

Ngugi wa Thiong'o (1977) *Petals of Blood*, London, Heinemann African Writers Series 188.

Ngugi wa Thiong'o (1978) *Homecoming: Essays on African and Caribbean Literature, Culture and Politics*, London, Heinemann Educational Books.

Niane, D. T. (1965) *Sundiata: An Epic of Old Mali*, Harlow, Longman.

Nkrumah, K. (1970) *Consciencism: Philosophy and Ideology for Decolonization*, London, Panaf Books.

Ovcharenko, A. (1978) *Socialist Realism and the Modern Literary Process*, Moscow, Progress Publishers.

Ousmane, S. C. (1976) *God's Bits of Wood*, London, Heinemann African Writers Series 63.

Paton, A. (1948) *Cry, the Beloved Country*, London, Longman edition 1966.

Progress Publishers (1974) *The Fundamentals of Marxist-Leninist Philosophy*, Moscow.

Schneider, E. V. (1957) *Industrial Sociology*, New York, McGraw-Hill.

Sithole, B. J. (1974) 'Politics is Character – in South Africa: An Assessment of the Influence of Politics on People's Characters as Shown in Two of Nadine Gordimer's Novels', Roma, Lesotho, UBLS BA Project.

Southall, R. (1977) *Literature, the Individual and Society*, London, Lawrence & Wishart.

Soyinka, W. (1973) *Season of Anomy*, London, Rex Collings.

Soyinka, W. (1978) *Myth, Literature and the African World*, Cambridge, Cambridge University Press.

Stuart, S. R. (1974) *Mao Tse-Tung Unrehearsed: Talks and letters 1956-1971*, Harmondsworth, Penguin.

Therborn, G. (1980) *The Ideology of Power and the Power of Ideology*, London, Verso.

Trotsky, L. (1960) *Literature and Revolution*, Ann Arbor, University of Michigan Press.

Vázquez, A. S. (1979) *Art and Society*, London, The Merlin Press.

Vinson, J. (ed.) (1972) *Contemporary Novelists*, London, St James Press.

Wauthier, C. (1978) *The Literature and Thought of Modern Africa*, London, Heinemann.

Williams, R. (1977) *Marxism and Literature*, Oxford, Oxford University Press.

Writers' Union of the USSR (1980) *Soviet Literature 1980*, No. 8, Moscow.

Zell, H. M. and Silver, H. (eds.) (1972) *A Reader's Guide to African Literature*, London, Heinemann. Zell, H. M., Bundy, C. and Coulon, V. (eds.) (1983) *A New Reader's Guide to African Literature*, London, Heinemann.

Index